MW00462996

Project Scheduling and Cost Control

Planning, Monitoring and Controlling the Baseline

James C. Taylor, PMP

Copyright ©2008 by J. Ross Publishing, Inc.

ISBN-10: 1-932159-11-8
ISBN-13: 978-1-932159-11-0

Printed and bound in the U.S.A. Printed on acid-free paper
10 9 8 7 6 5 4 3 2 1

Library of Congress Cataloging-in-Publication Data

Taylor, James, 1937-
    Project scheduling and cost control : planning, monitoring and controlling
the baseline / by James Taylor.
        p. cm.
    Includes index.
    ISBN-10: 1-932159-11-8
    ISBN-13: 978-1-932159-11-0 (hardcover : alk. paper)
    1. Project management. 2. Production scheduling. 3. Cost control. I.
Title.
    HD69.P75.T3884 2007
    658.4′04—dc22   2007030826

Phone: (954) 727-9333
Fax: (561) 892-0700
Web: www.jrosspub.com

DEDICATION

To Taylor Ashton Bailey,
my first grandchild and surely
the most beautiful young lady on this planet

TABLE OF CONTENTS

PREFACE

Projects fail most often because of poorly written or misinterpreted requirements. But once a project is begun, controlling schedule and cost is the most difficult aspect of the project manager's job. I have wanted to write a book on schedule and cost control for many years, but other projects and my teaching schedule have delayed this dream. Now, however, I have finally managed to collect what I think are the most important aspects of schedule and cost control in one place—this book.

I also have tried to make this a practical book on project management principles, tools, and techniques by explaining the complex in as simple a fashion as possible and by incorporating many templates and examples of how all these tools work. Most project managers want prescriptive directions about how to run a successful project; that really is not possible. If project management were prescriptive, then the process of managing a project would become simply an administrative task. Yet we certainly can make the process practicable inasmuch as the tools provided can aid the project manager today; that is, all the principles, tools, and techniques discussed in this book can be applied as soon as the project manager returns to his or her office. That is my objective.

There are several books on the market that address the problem of schedule and cost control, and you might wonder: Why another book on the subject? I do not think a practicing, professional project manager can read or learn too much on the subject. Read everything you can get your hands on and use the tips and ideas from all those sources that most improve your expertise and performance. I have tried, in this book, to address what seem to be—based upon extensive conversations with many practicing project managers and my many students and my own 38 years of experience as a project manager—the most challenging project management issues and to clarify the problems associated with these issues. Furthermore, I have arranged the book in the order that most of these schedule and cost control issues occur as a project manager and his or her team progress through the life cycle of a project.

The first chapter introduces the subject of schedule and cost control and discusses in more detail why it is needed. Then the most challenging of project management issues—requirements development—is immediately addressed in Chapter 2. Once the requirements are developed, understood, and agreed upon by all stakeholders, the next step in the project process is to describe the project scope through the development of the work breakdown structure, from which the cost and schedule baselines can be developed. This process is fully described in Chapter 3.

Because developing costs is so crucial and difficult, I have included two chapters on the subject; Chapter 4 describes cost estimating generally, and Chapter 5 provides significant detail about the different cost categories a project manager must be aware of and also provides significant detail about what is important when assessing one contract bid against another.

Chapter 6 then discusses schedule development. Many professional project managers insist that the budget should be set before the schedule is developed. That usually is not possible since most customers have an operational need to field the deliverable by a particular date. Therefore, the schedule is usually the driving force behind budget development. However, for the most part, schedule and cost development is an iterative process with the objective of optimizing both. Hence, my personal practice is to develop the two together. Chapter 6 describes the process of developing the schedule, but the reader should consider Chapters 4, 5, and 6 as one group that is necessary for developing budgets and schedules.

The next logical step in preparing to implement a project is the planning phase, which is discussed in Chapter 7. Chapters 8 and 9 also should be considered as one unit; Chapter 8 discusses general implementation procedures and issues, while Chapter 9 discusses earned value management, which is the preferred approach to monitoring and controlling the progress of a project. I opted to separate these topics in order to place proper emphasis on the earned value methodology, but the two chapters can be considered as the implementation phase of a project.

Finally, Chapter 10 discusses the project closing process. The closing phase of a project is often the most difficult phase because all the team members are being pulled away from the project to begin work on new projects. But the closing phase is all-important because this is the time the customer accepts or does not accept the project deliverables, which, of course, are the reason for the project in the first place.

I have also been careful to write this book so that everything in it is consistent with the Project Management Institute's standards. Where there are differences between PMI®'s approach and my own opinion, I so note. Having said that, the final objective of this book is, first, to instruct the project manager who needs help in controlling project costs and schedules and, second, to provide additional instruction for those who are preparing to take their Project Management Professional (PMP®) certification exam. It is my hope that this book will be a good reference for PMP® certification.

Jim Taylor
Peachtree City, Georgia

ABOUT THE AUTHOR

James C. Taylor is a certified Project Management Professional (PMP®) with over 39 years of highly diversified experience in project and program management, marketing, and business development in both the public and private sectors. His principal experience is in the information technology and engineering training industries and includes the design and development of flight simulator equipment and computer-based flight-training courses for the U.S. military.

Mr. Taylor has taught graduate courses in project management, leadership, and negotiation skills and strategies at Marymount University in Virginia and in project management at George Washington University in Washington, D.C. He has designed, developed, and taught numerous core and IT project management courses as well as contracting courses for project managers. He also was previously the Senior Advisor at ESI International, the world's largest provider of project management training, and actively managed the development and update of all of ESI's project management courses. He has been an active speaker over the years and has authored numerous articles and books in the field of project management.

Mr. Taylor has a B.S. in mathematics and a B.S. and M.S. in aerospace engineering from Auburn University, an M.S. in organizational development from Marymount University, and a D.Sc. (all but dissertation) in engineering from George Washington University. He is a consultant in project management and project management training. Mr. Taylor lives in Peachtree City, Georgia.

ACKNOWLEDGMENTS

I have been either practicing or teaching project management for over 38 years. It is impossible to mention all those who have been my teachers and mentors, but I want to thank you all. I have been blessed to have had teachers and mentors who were excellent project managers, and all of them constantly and patiently shared their knowledge and experience with me. This book comes not so much from my independent thinking but rather from the collective experience, knowledge, and thinking of the many who have guided me in a long and successful project management career. For that, I'll always be grateful.

But mostly I want to acknowledge all the students whom I have taught over the years. Surely, the best way to learn is to teach, and all my students continue to challenge me intellectually and professionally. I can't imagine a better way to finish my career than to impart whatever knowledge and experience I have to others. And I look forward to every day as an opportunity to meet and help another project management student.

Free value-added materials available from
the Download Resource Center at www.jrosspub.com

At J. Ross Publishing we are committed to providing today's professional with practical, hands-on tools that enhance the learning experience and give readers an opportunity to apply what they have learned. That is why we offer free ancillary materials available for download on this book and all participating Web Added Value™ publications. These online resources may include interactive versions of material that appears in the book or supplemental templates, worksheets, models, plans, case studies, proposals, spreadsheets and assessment tools, among other things. Whenever you see the WAV™ symbol in any of our publications, it means bonus materials accompany the book and are available from the Web Added Value Download Resource Center at www.jrosspub.com.

Downloads available for *Project Scheduling and Cost Control: Planning, Monitoring, and Controlling the Baseline* consist of scheduling and cost control templates and a slide presentation highlighting critical points related to these components.

INTRODUCTION

The reason most often cited for project failure is that requirements are not clearly defined or stated or that they are misinterpreted. Consequently, every study of schedule and cost control typically begins by describing needs and requirements and how to ensure they are accurately presented and interpreted. In that regard, this book is similar. What is different about this book is that, in addition to describing requirements and requirements analyses in detail, it discusses how to incorporate these requirements into a project plan and how to set up and implement a monitoring and control system to ensure that projects are successfully completed on time and on budget.

This book describes processes, tools, and techniques necessary and available to manage any project. The terminology, tools, and techniques generally will not be new to someone who has any project management experience, but they are presented so that the members of a project team—even those who have little experience—can apply them immediately to better implement, monitor, and control their projects.

THE NATURE OF SCHEDULE AND COST CONTROL

Before describing ways of monitoring and controlling projects, there are two questions about schedule and cost control that need to be asked and answered:

1. *What* is schedule and cost control?
2. *Why* do we need schedule and cost control?

What Is Schedule and Cost Control?

Schedule and cost control encompasses four aspects or elements of project work that are primary concerns for the project manager and his or her team:

- Directing progress
- Directing actions
- Controlling results
- Conserving resources

Directing Progress

This element of project management refers to the efforts involved in directing the progress of a project against the project plan, particularly in regard to those efforts that impact the cost, schedule, and scope. Almost everything the project team does—every decision that is made—potentially affects one or all of these three components. Cost, for example, affects both schedule and scope, schedule affects cost and scope, and scope affects cost and schedule. Accordingly, if the schedule slips, then it costs more to bring the project back to its original planned timeline, or if the schedule must be met, the customer may prefer to modify the scope by eliminating some of the functionality of the product. Simply stated, directing progress in a way that minimizes negative impacts or directing progress to take advantage of positive impacts is the key to successful project management.

Directing Actions

Directing actions involves taking the proper action to minimize the variances between the planned and actual progress. If, for example, a project is determined to be over budget, then some action is required to bring the spending back into line with the planned budget. Sometimes the action will require some adjustment to the schedule or to the scope, but every action will have a ripple effect; other components of the project will be affected, requiring additional action.

Controlling Results

Controlling results means being cognizant of the fact that any action taken must have a strategy or tactic to control the impact to the project as a whole and to the other components of schedule, cost, and scope. There is no gain if an action taken pushes the project in an unchecked direction. Being able to predict and control the results of the actions taken will ultimately move the project back to its planned track if it is determined that there is some variance from the original plan.

Conserving Resources

Conserving or controlling resources is the one element of project management that causes the project manager the most grief. There almost never are enough resources available to implement and run a project properly. Therefore, the project manager is responsible for apportioning and conserving resources in the most optimal way possible. Otherwise, the project is doomed before it ever begins.

Why Do We Need Schedule and Cost Control?

The problems of keeping a project on track by directing and controlling the impacts to scope (deliverables, quality), cost (resources, budget), and schedule (activities, time) were mentioned in the previous section. These three elements make up what is known as the *triple constraint,* shown in Figure 1.1. The triple constraint typically is shown as a triangle because each facet

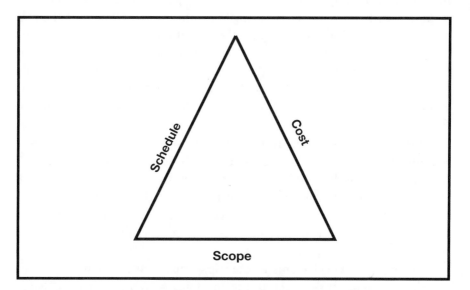

FIGURE 1.1.   The Project Management Triple Constraint Triangle

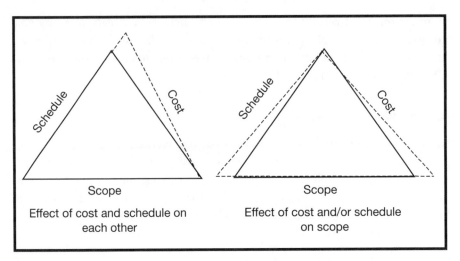

Effect of cost and schedule on each other

Effect of cost and/or schedule on scope

FIGURE 1.2. Effect of Project Management Triangle Component Changes

is critical; none is more important than the others, at least in terms of project control. When one component of the triangle is changed, almost invariably one or both of the others changes.

The triple constraint is a useful view of important components of project management. It is often referred to as the project management triple constraint. The three elements encapsulate a total project. If one of them is changed, then at least one of the others is affected; often both are. For example, if a project goes over budget, scope may have to be decreased to get the project back on the budget plan. If a project is behind schedule (time), more resources may have to be added to get it back on schedule, but adding resources means added costs. These change effects are illustrated in Figure 1.2.

In the left triangle in Figure 1.2, it is clear that if the schedule increases, then the costs must increase because of the additional resources to accommodate or reduce the schedule overrun. Often the reverse is true: if there is an increase in costs, the schedule must be extended to reduce the number of resources needed. The right triangle shows that to reduce the schedule and the costs back to the original estimates, the scope of the project must be reduced.

Keeping the three elements of the triple constraint in balance is one of the aims of a project manager and team; doing so is a juggling act that is sometimes very difficult and requires a good grasp of a number of management skills, such as communication, risk management, contracting, reporting, team building, selling, and many others.

To summarize the three aspects of the triple constraint triangle, the following may be useful in understanding the exact meaning of each of the sides:

- **Scope**—The *PMBOK® Guide* defines scope as the *sum of the products and services to be provided.* In other words, project scope is the work to be done in a project to meet project requirements.
- **Cost**—The money, labor, equipment, and other resources needed to complete a project.
- **Schedule**—The time it takes to complete a project or to reach intermediate points or milestones within an overall project.

The concept of the triple constraint is used early in the planning stages of a project to understand the customer's needs and to consider how each factor interacts with the others and how together they contribute to the whole project. The triple constraint is also useful during the course of a project in dealing with changes, contingencies, risks, assumptions, replanning, and issues that may arise. In short, every process, every phase, and every activity of project management are all performed against the backdrop of the triple constraint.

THE PROJECT LIFE CYCLE

Every project has a life cycle that is comparable to a biological life cycle in that it begins slowly and quickly builds as the project work starts to produce deliverables. As a project reaches its final days, activity slows down and tapers off. A project life cycle shows the project effort (and costs) as the work takes place and maps this over time, often shown as a graphic.

There are no standard life cycle models. Each industry uses its own model, and variations of the model are found even within an industry. Moreover, the names used for the phases in each model are not always the same; the names differ from industry to industry or even according to an organization's preference. For example, one organization may refer to the first phase as the initiation phase whereas another may call it the concept phase; some industries use four life cycle phases for their projects, whereas others use seven or more phases. Regardless of what the phases are named or how many exist, the project management activities and the tools and techniques available are generally very much the same across all industries.

In the life cycle model in Figure 1.3, the five phases are *concept, planning, design and development, implementation,* and *closeout.* Each of these phases has its own subphases, steps, or stages, and these usually are defined by an organization to suit the way it defines and develops its projects. Generally, the activities for each phase can be described as:

- Concept
- Planning
- Design and development
- Implementation
- Closeout

Concept

This is the data-gathering phase. The project is just beginning, and who the project manager and team members are has not yet been determined. (Note that there has usually been a previous phase to select the project; in almost every case, a project manager is not involved in project selection. Rather, a project is handed to the project manager after decisions have been made to pursue the project and for what purposes.) During the concept phase, the project manager will determine, to the best extent possible, what the requirements are and what the resource commitment needs to be.

Planning

The planning phase takes the concept phase into the details of planning, where the requirements definition is more specifically developed, a work breakdown structure is prepared, schedule and cost estimates are developed, and the project plan is written. It is also the phase during which the project team is organized.

Design and Development

Blueprinting of the project occurs in this phase. The project manager conducts design meetings as needed to gather all information necessary to create

Concept	Planning	Design and Development	Implementation	Closeout
■ Gather data ■ Identify need ■ Establish: □ Goals, objectives □ Basic economics, feasibility □ Stakeholders □ Risk level □ Strategy □ Potential team ■ Guesstimate resources ■ Identify alternatives ■ Present proposal ■ Obtain approval for next phase	■ Appoint key team members ■ Conduct studies ■ Develop scope baseline: □ End product(s) □ Quality standards □ Resources □ Activities ■ Establish: □ Master plan □ Budget, cash flow □ Work breakdown structure □ Policies and procedures ■ Assess risks ■ Confirm justification ■ Present project brief ■ Obtain approval to proceed	■ Set up: □ Organization □ Communications ■ Motivate team ■ Detail technical requirements ■ Establish: □ Work packages □ Information control systems ■ Procure goods and services ■ Execute work packages	■ Direct/monitor/forecast/control: □ Scope □ Quality □ Time □ Cost ■ Resolve problems	■ Finalize product(s) ■ Review and accept ■ Settle final accounts ■ Transfer product responsibility ■ Evaluate project ■ Document results ■ Release/redirect resources ■ Reassign project team

FIGURE 1.3. A Project Life Cycle

the design documents. The project manager, subject matter experts, and other stakeholders must review and approve the design document before development begins. The actual work on the project deliverables, or project products, starts and takes place during this phase. The key functions of scheduling and cost control occur here, inasmuch as variances from the plan (or baseline) are measured and control strategies are implemented to keep actual progress as close to the plan as practical.

Implementation

The implementation of the project deliverables, or project products, takes place during this phase. The project manager continues to monitor variances from the plan and implement strategies to keep the project on course. Any problems need to be resolved in order to achieve a successful closeout.

Closeout

This is often the most difficult phase because a project manager loses team members to other projects as the current project in seen to be winding down. Furthermore, many organizations do not support the activities of this phase as strongly as they should because they are moving on to other projects. Yet this phase is critical to the success of a project in a way different from all other phases: this is the phase that delivers the final efforts to customers. It is concerned with conducting a scope review to determine that everything planned (or promised) has been accomplished and delivered, obtaining customer acceptance of deliverables, and closing out administrative and contractual paperwork. It is also the time to develop lessons learned documentation, without which process improvement is made less effective.

REQUIREMENTS REVIEW

Reviewing what is involved in developing requirements is important and adds value. A frequently mentioned reason for project failure is poorly stated or unclear requirements. Moreover, even with clearly stated requirements, the project team can misinterpret what the customer means or wants.

Writing clear requirements is truly an art. We can all think of the many instances when we thought we understood a person to say one thing when in fact he or she said or meant something else entirely. Therefore, it is always wise to list all the requirements as they are understood and then reexamine each one with the customer to ensure nothing has been missed and to get the customer's agreement that the requirements have been interpreted correctly.

The requirements review is also the time to identify the project stakeholders. *Stakeholders* are those people or organizations that have an interest in a project, are affected by some or all of a project's activities, or, by virtue of their positions, can make or break a project. A serious mistake that inexperienced project managers often make is overlooking those people or organizations that think they are stakeholders, even though they may not fit the strict definition of the term. If in doubt, it is far better to include a person or organization in the stakeholder analysis than to exclude a possible stakeholder that may have the power to negatively affect the project if they feel left out or snubbed.

Of course, the real reason for doing requirements analyses is to determine what needs to be accomplished. However, just as importantly, without a complete understanding of the requirements, it is impossible to develop the cost, time (schedule), and scope targets, which are the baselines against which project progress will be measured.

Finally, when performing a requirements review, it is imperative that the project manager includes acceptance criteria and obtains sign-off on these from the customer. *Acceptance criteria* are a statement of what will be used to conclude whether the project meets its desired outcomes or objectives. Without a mutual and agreed understanding of the "measuring sticks" for completion, the project manager cannot ascertain when the project activities are actually complete. As such, a project could easily become never-ending.

SCHEDULE AND COST CONTROL DOCUMENTATION

The basis for a solid scheduling and cost control system is to use some key tools. As with any aspect of project management, the development of good analyses, detailed documentation, and accurate estimates (to the extent possible) is key to successfully completing a project.

In the case of schedule and cost control, some particularly useful documentation tools can add good value and should be kept in mind for use throughout a project and especially during the planning process. These documents include:

- Project charter
- Scope statement
- Project requirements document
- Work breakdown structure
- Time and cost estimates
- Responsibility matrix
- Risk management plan
- Change control process plan

Project Charter

The project charter is signed by the senior manager who has functional authority over all the resources and organizations working on a project. The principal function of the project charter is to name the project manager and authorize him or her to lead the project. The project manager usually prepares the project charter because he or she knows more about the project than anyone else. However, a senior manager signs it, and usually all the functional managers who have joint responsibility for supporting a project also sign it. An example of a project charter format is depicted in Figure 1.4.

Scope Statement

The scope statement describes a project and its purpose. Depending upon what other documentation accompanies a project (such as a contract, specifications, and engineering drawings), the scope statement can range in detail from a high-level statement of the work to a complete description of the project requirements.

Project Requirements Document

The project requirements document or PRD (depicted in Figure 1.5) is a document used to identify each of the requirements, assumptions, deliverables, and constraints, as well as several other pertinent facts. Because senior managers also sign the PRD, many people are confused about why it is necessary to sign off on both the project charter and the PRD. To simplify this distinction, the project charter deals with people, that is, *who* is performing the project; the PRD, on the other hand, deals with *what* the project is about. Therefore, senior management should sign both documents to formalize the

PROJECT CHARTER			
Project Name:	Project Ref./ID No.:	Preparer Name:	Preparer Signature:
Customer:	Customer Contact:	Contact Phone:	Date Prepared:

To (distribution):

From (initiating authority):

Assignment (include project manager's name, name of the project, customer's name):

Project Manager's Responsibility (describe the extent of the project manager's responsibility relative to planning, implementing, and delivering the project's product[s] or service[s]):

Project Manager's Authority (describe the level of project manager authority and the mechanisms and trigger points for escalating project issues to higher authority):

Functional Support (list all functional organizations and describe their responsibilities to the project):

Project Scope (briefly describe the scope and how the project supports the organization's strategic plan):

Authorizing Signature	Title	Date

FIGURE 1.4.   Project Charter Format

PROJECT REQUIREMENTS DOCUMENT			
Project Name:	Project Ref. No.:	Preparer Name:	Preparer Signature:
Customer:	Customer Contact:	Contact Phone:	Date Prepared:

Project Summary/Background

Project Objectives/Deliverables

Key Milestones

Assumptions and Constraints

Risks

Key Resource Requirements

Acceptance Criteria

Interrelated Projects

Reviews

Communications Plan

Change Management Plan

Financial Analysis

Signatures

FIGURE 1.5.   Project Requirements Document Format

authority of the project manager and to indicate organizational commitment to performing the project.

Work Breakdown Structure

The work breakdown structure (WBS) is way to decompose a project into its lowest components and is the single most important tool in a project manager's tool kit. Decomposing a project into a WBS framework can be accomplished in two ways: the indented format and the graphic or tree format. These formats are depicted in Figures 3.2 and 3.3, respectively, where the WBS is discussed in detail.

With a fully developed and detailed WBS, every other tool can be developed and a project plan can be created. In short, the WBS is the basis for schedule and cost control. A WBS can be developed with either a product-oriented or a task-oriented focus, and one should be very careful about how each is used.

The product-oriented WBS has its place in high-level estimating, for communication purposes, or for beginning to understand a high-tech project by starting off with its deliverables. When it is necessary to accurately estimate schedules and costs as well as to manage a project, a WBS needs to be developed in detail, showing the task or the work package level.

Time and Cost Estimates

Time and cost estimates rightly follow the WBS because a network analysis (using precedence diagramming, discussed later) can be developed from the WBS and lead to final schedules. A project can have many schedules: a master schedule, task schedules, milestones, meetings and reports, and so on. After a practical schedule is developed, then the cost of the project can be determined.

Responsibility Matrix

The responsibility matrix serves several purposes. First, it documents who is responsible for each task in lead, approval, and support positions. Second, it is a handy management tool for keeping track of who is doing what task and is particularly useful as a "management by walking around" document. Third, it is a good communication tool. During status briefings or as a supplement to status reports, it shows which stakeholders are responsible for various project tasks.

Risk Management Plan

The risk management plan is one of many plans that are part of the project plan, but it is highlighted here because it is the most important of all ancillary plans. Risk analysis and planning begin with the WBS and are performed throughout the entire life of a project. Without good risk planning, a project is more exposed and has an increased likelihood of failure.

Change Control Process Plan

The purpose of change control in general is to control scope creep; without it, scope creep is inevitable. *Scope creep* usually occurs when customers or other stakeholders want to add small enhancements to a project. However, unless these changes are made in a formalized fashion, scope will grow (creep) without an attendant increase in schedule (time) or budget (cost). (Recall the triple constraint.) Change control is a vital part of scope management, and available forms assist in the overall change control process (discussed in greater detail in Chapter 10).

Others

The "art" side of project management dictates that project managers must determine what tools, techniques, documents, or other aids are available and required to successfully control the schedule, cost, and scope baselines. Thus, as you gain experience in project management, you will find there are many other documentation tools that will make your job easier, adding to your ability to successfully complete a project. Unfortunately, there is no prescription for success in project management—only suggestions and a few important tips. There are other aids that you are bound to discover for yourself.

SUMMARY

Over half of all new projects fail. The concept of schedule and cost control is not new, and it should not come as a surprise that all organizations, whether or not they employ project management practices in their business, are concerned about controlling work so that it meets its schedule and cost objectives.

The WBS is the most important tool for defining and developing schedule and cost control systems. With a well-developed WBS, every other project management tool can be developed. In short, it is the basis of schedule and cost control.

REFERENCES OF INTEREST

Kerzner, Harold. *Project Management: A Systems Approach to Planning, Scheduling, and Controlling.* 8th ed. New York: Wiley, 2003.

Meredith, Jack R., and Samuel J. Mantel, Jr. *Project Management: A Managerial Approach.* 5th ed. New York: Wiley, 1995.

2

IDENTIFYING AND DEVELOPING CUSTOMER REQUIREMENTS

More than half of the errors in a project originate with the requirements and analysis activities done prior to product design. Requirements are the heart of any project. They describe what the outcome of a project must be, what it must do, or the qualities it must have. In order to be successful, the project manager and his or her team need to identify and manage the project requirements. However, knowing that one must identify and manage requirements and actually doing so are two different things. Most projects fail as a result of incomplete requirements, poorly written requirements, or misinterpreted requirements.

Requirements are generated or elicited from current systems, end users, and other key stakeholders. They generally come from the customer and describe a need. However, requirements are generated not only as a result of stated needs but also due to organizational needs for technical or business capabilities.

Too many people think of the fulfillment of requirements as applying only to outcomes that are *tangible* products. The best way to think of a project outcome, however, is to ask: *What is the end result of this project?* The answer may be a product, but it can also be a service or even a new procedure or process improvement. Understanding the purpose of a project makes it easier to identify the requirements, which is not always an easy task.

Obviously, many other areas must be addressed and resolved in project management. This chapter focuses on the number one problem project managers face: understanding, identifying, and managing requirements.

WHO DEFINES REQUIREMENTS?

Not all projects have completely definable requirements all the time. In fact, many projects, particularly those involving new or cutting-edge technology, may start with only general ideas about the purpose of the end product. In these instances, it is appropriate to develop the system requirements as the project progresses. However, even under these circumstances, and perhaps even more so, the requirements definition process has to be disciplined, documented, and scrupulously followed.

The customer defines requirements. That is, the customer, whether internal to an organization or external, desires a product or a service to meet some need and then communicates this need to the provider. The problem is that the customer often cannot describe precisely what is being requested. Sometimes the product may be too cutting edge to even understand fully its functional capabilities, or the customer may know exactly what is needed but may not be able to communicate the requirements clearly.

To make matters worse, the producing organization may not have a process for identifying and analyzing requirements—and thus may be incapable of correctly interpreting them even when they are clearly communicated. In addition, the producing organization may not have a sophisticated enough process to accurately relate customer requirements to organizational strategic and business needs.

WHAT ARE REQUIREMENTS AND WHY DO WE NEED THEM?

At the most basic level in project management, it should be understood that the customer or buyer establishes requirements usually as a result of some operational need. Equally important, however, is that the provider organization also has a need to improve its capability, competitiveness, or dominance in a particular area. Hence, some requirements are the result of the provider organization's strategic objectives and may be driven by a company's need to improve or change its core business.

A specific requirement is something a product (or service) must do or a quality a product must have. Any requirement exists primarily because the customer wants the product to have a particular functionality or quality. A requirement also can exist simply because the product type demands certain functions or qualities. For example, to be truly functional, a product that is used in testing might need to be self-aligning or self-calibrating to a preset tolerance. Hence, a secondary requirement to self-align is inherent in the functional capability of the product because of the primary requirement to test rapidly, often, and accurately.

Most of us can readily accept that a product must have certain functional requirements, but many of us do not realize that there also are nonfunctional requirements. Understanding the different types of requirements is crucial to identifying and planning to meet them.

Project managers and their teams need requirements definition from the customer in order to accurately define, plan for, and deliver the product or service the customer needs. Without requirements, there is no project.

TYPES OF REQUIREMENTS

Assuming the customer defines the requirements accurately and completely, the project manager must also understand—and be able to identify—the different types of requirements, which complicates the project manager's job. Basically, there are two types of requirements: functional and nonfunctional. However, there is another type that is often overlooked: generated or hidden requirements.

Functional Requirements

A functional requirement is one that a product must have in order to provide the capability needed by the ultimate user. Actually, functional requirements are the fundamental basis for a product in the first place. If a product does not perform a function, do a job, or complete a task, then the need for it is eliminated.

The following is an example of a functional requirement statement:

> The product shall produce an amended resource availability roster at the end of every work shift.

To be serviceable to the user, this product must provide the capability of keeping track of and reporting on the available resources each time a work shift comes to an end.

Generally, a description provided by the customer will yield several and even hundreds of functional requirements, depending upon the complexity of the product. For every functional requirement, however, there also can be one or more nonfunctional requirements.

Nonfunctional Requirements

A nonfunctional requirement is a quality or property that a product must have. Sometimes this type of requirement is critical to the success of a product, but often a nonfunctional requirement simply enhances the look of a product or in other ways identifies a product as something unique to an organization. Nonetheless, it is a requirement and it is important to the customer—sometimes even more important than a functional requirement.

The following is an example of a nonfunctional requirement:

> The Essex Company logo will be prominently displayed on the front of the product.

This requirement—displaying the company's logo—clearly does not affect the functionality of the product. The product will work regardless of whether the logo is present. To the Essex Company, however, prominence of the logo may be of significant marketing importance, particularly if the product is critical to an operation and its contribution is seen by hundreds of people.

Consider, for example, the timing equipment at the Olympics games. As important as the accuracy and reliability of the equipment are, it is just as important, to the provider at least, that its name be prominently displayed on or with the equipment.

Nonfunctional requirements are often overlooked during the requirements identification process, or if not overlooked, they are considered less important and not given the appropriate attention. This negligence can be catastrophic.

Hidden or Generated Requirements

Hidden or generated requirements are those that are generated in order to accomplish another requirement, usually in the provider organization. For example, a stated required functional capability by the customer may be beyond the technical capabilities of the provider organization. Hence, to meet the requirement, the provider must either develop the requisite capability, hire experts that can provide the capability, or team with another company or hire a vendor to provide the expertise.

The obvious answer to eliminating problems resulting from requirements interpretation is for the customer to establish clear and concise requirements and for the provider to ensure they are precisely interpreted. But how are these actions brought together to yield the desired result? There are three key steps: a clearly written set of requirements, a medium for transmitting these requirements to the provider, and a process for ensuring the provider and the customer are in complete agreement about the intent of the project and the results desired. The first step is to provide a clearly written set of requirements.

WRITING REQUIREMENTS

Written requirements are expected when the customer is external to an organization. If an organization lives or dies by its ability to bid for contracts (as in the defense industry, for example), it would be inconceivable that written requirements would not be provided in the form of a statement of work (SOW). When the customer is internal to an organization, it is more likely that a written description of the desired product or service not only will not be provided but also will not even be considered. Whether the customer is external or internal to an organization, all projects should have written requirements, and each internal project should be viewed and managed just as if it is governed by a binding contract. The reasons will become clear in the following sections.

The best requirements-writing guides are the requirements or specification documents from previous successfully completed projects. An organization's "lessons learned" archives quickly yield the basic elements for developing a working template for writing the next project SOW. Some tips for describing requirements and developing a good SOW are given in Figure 2.1.

1. **Describe the work**—Describe all the work to be done as completely, clearly, and concisely as possible.

2. **Do not dictate how to do the work**—Write a functional description of the desired product or service when possible.

3. **Clearly differentiate requirements**—Describe only one requirement per requirement statement.

4. **Avoid ambiguous statements and words**—Avoid words or phrases that do not have exact meanings.

5. **Repeat the statement of requirements for clarity and legality**—If requirements are embedded in other documents attached to the contract, repeat them in the SOW or include them by reference.

6. **Include illustrations, tables, charts, and diagrams**—Include anything in the SOW that aids in understanding the requirements.

7. **Flow down requirements**—Pass on any requirements from prime contracts to subcontracts. Requirements imposed on the prime provider by the customer must be included in the vendor's SOW for the vendor's area of work responsibility.

8. **Always have the statement of work reviewed/critiqued by others**—A review by an objective reader will reveal how clearly the SOW is written.

FIGURE 2.1. Tips for Writing Good Statements of Work

Writing a good SOW—that is, developing a project requirement statement—is an art and is the ultimate test of a good writer. A requirement should be written in as simple language as possible and should be stated in one sentence. If describing a requirement takes more than one sentence or requires two or more verbs and/or conjunctions, then there are probably two or more requirements in the statement.

Consider the following requirement statement:

The product shall be capable of testing 300 samples per hour and shall print test results on a standard-size sheet of paper (8.5 by 11 inches) in a two-column, tabular format.

There are actually two requirements in this statement. The first deals with how many samples the product must test per hour, and the second addresses the test report characteristics. The point here is that whether writing or interpreting requirements, it is important that they be completely differentiated to avoid overlooking one or more of them.

THE STATEMENT OF WORK

We have discussed that the customer develops and writes requirements as a part of the SOW, but have not yet discussed precisely what this document is. The SOW is the second step in bringing the customer and the provider to an understanding of the purpose of the project. In short, the SOW is how the requirements are transmitted to the provider. It basically defines the project scope and is the communication medium in the process of defining a project.

An SOW is most often associated with a request for proposal, which is the formal document issued by a buying organization inviting potential offerors to bid on a contract. However, organizations need to practice writing SOWs for their internal projects as well. As we shall see, the SOW is a definitive description of the work, and having such a document can only aid the project team in fulfilling the desires of the customer, whether internal or external.

There are several reasons why an SOW is critical to project success. First, this is the document that completely describes the work to be done. Second, the SOW describes what constitutes "acceptance." That is, the SOW should always contain a section that describes what the project team must do to provide an acceptable product or service and, likewise, how the customer will measure when the project is complete. Unless this completion criterion is explicitly stated in the SOW, the project may never be completed because the customer can always claim the deliverable did not meet the intended desires or needs. Third, the SOW takes precedence over all other documents. For instance, if a specification attached to the SOW describes the desired functionality of the product differently than the SOW describes it, the SOW is the document that must be followed. Of course, the discrepancy between the two documents should be pointed out to the customer for clarification and possible amendment. However, the essential point is that many providers will have assumed that, for instance, the engineering specification describing the product is precisely what has to be delivered, only to find themselves redoing the product, at company expense, because the SOW described something slightly different.

For smaller, less costly projects, the buyer might issue a specification or a needs statement. The difference is in the amount of detail, but whatever term is used to describe the customer's needs, the purpose is the same: to describe the needs of the customer. In this book, we will concentrate on the SOW because that is the most difficult and most detailed of the needs descriptions. However, even SOWs can take on a different focus or amount of detail depending on the type of SOW used to describe a particular project.

Types of Statements of Work

There are three major types of SOWs:

- Design or detailed specification
- Level of effort
- Performance oriented

Although there are other types and variations of each of these, these three generally meet the needs of most projects.

Design or Detailed Specification Statement of Work

A design or detailed specification SOW tells the provider how to do the work. It may include precise measurements, tolerances, materials, quality control requirements, and any other specific constraints determined to be important to the customer.

There are definite advantages and disadvantages to this type of SOW. Some of the advantages are:

- The customer is able to describe precisely what is required and how it is to be built.
- There generally is less potential for misinterpreting the customer's requirements.
- The provider is relieved of bearing the risk for the project.
- Up-front efforts are generally reduced. That is, generally less design and less testing of various technical solutions are required.

The disadvantages of this type of SOW are:

- The customer must bear the major risk burden for the project because the customer is dictating the solution and how it is to be provided. When the customer provides too much detail in the specifications or in the description of a requirement, then the customer is defining or "forcing" a solution.
- The customer may not get the most cost-effective or most functional product since this approach precludes evaluation of other solutions.
- It generally produces poor projects in the information technology world because it dampens or even eliminates creativity.

This type of SOW is generally used in a manufacturing or construction business, but other work efforts are often described in this format. It can be used to good effect in the information technology environment, but it should be used discriminatingly and only for small, highly defined projects. Otherwise, the very essence of any high-tech creativity is compromised.

Level-of-Effort Statement of Work

The level-of-effort SOW is an excellent type of SOW that is used effectively in practically any type of service industry or project. A level-of-effort SOW can be written for almost any type of service unless it is an inherent organizational service. The real deliverable under this type of effort is an hour of work. That is, the customer contracts for time and pays the provider according to the amount of time spent providing the task. Usually, this type of contract has a weekly or monthly cap on the amount of compensated work, which requires the provider to closely control the amount of scheduled work. The provider generally has to produce proof, in the form of certified time sheets, to the customer before payment is made. This type of SOW can also be used within an organization to track how much effort is expended in accomplishing such projects as upgrades to managerial systems control processes.

Performance-Based Statement of Work

The most efficient and effective SOW model is the performance-based SOW. The performance-based SOW is always the preferred method for transmitting the customer's needs because it structures all aspects of an acquisition around the purpose of the work and not around how to accomplish the work. This approach has a number of advantages for both the customer and the provider. The two most important advantages are:

1. The provider or contractor has the freedom to develop and evaluate different solutions to meet the customer's requirements.
2. The customer can concentrate on obtaining the desired provider instead of the provider's processes.

This approach usually costs less than the design or detailed specification SOW because the focus is on functionality rather than meeting precise engineering measurements. That is, it is generally more important that a desired result is obtained from turning a knob than it is that the knob be turned precisely one-quarter turn to obtain the result. The cost of engineering the latter example is significantly higher than designing for functionality.

It is possible that some combination of SOW types may be needed. For example, an information technology project that is part of a satellite communications system must of necessity contain specifications that describe close engineering tolerances. Likewise, satellite size and weight constraints are described in the SOW and accompanying documents, but many of the other project requirements are described in terms of the functions the system must perform.

Benefits of a Well-Written Statement of Work

The SOW, as the most essential document in any solicitation, contract, or important internal project initiative, must be written so that all technical and nontechnical readers can understand it. But writing a good SOW is not easy. It requires close attention to detail and a thorough understanding of the need.

The investment of time and effort to write a clear and high-quality SOW:

■ Enables offerors or internal project teams to understand clearly the customer's requirements and needs
■ Allows project teams to more accurately schedule and cost the effort and to develop a higher quality technical solution to meet the requirement

- Minimizes the need for change orders or other project adjustments, which increase project cost and usually schedule duration
- Provides a milieu for establishing performance and completion criteria
- Provides both the customer and the project team a way to assess performance and progress
- Reduces claims and disputes in a contracted effort

The Statement of Work Format

The SOW can be thought of as the project specification. Although many SOWs will contain engineering specifications, usually as attachments or appendices, many will not, nor should they. This is especially true of SOWs that have been prepared as performance-based documents. Thinking of the SOW as a specification, however, gives an added emphasis to the importance of the document, if there is still any doubt. This thinking also helps focus the writer's attention on providing clear and concise descriptions of the work, and it helps focus the reader on the salient points of the document.

There are several SOW format variations that are effective and useful, but generally all SOWs have the same basic sections. A general format is provided in Figure 2.2. The SOW format is straightforward, but the section on scope is described below as a guide to the type of detail expected in each of the sections.

Scope

The scope section is really an introduction to the project. In one sense, the word is a little misleading because we think of the SOW as providing the project "scope," so it is logical to assume that the scope section would do exactly that. However, this section is simply a high-level statement of what is described in the rest of the SOW and generally what the project is about.

The following is an example of the scope section:

> This Statement of Work defines the effort required for the design, engineering development, software programming, fabrication, and test of a prototype of the (*Project Name*) Information Technology System to determine system feasibility. It includes the associated project management, human engineering, and logistics support planning requirements.

I. Scope
II. Background
III. Applicable Documents
IV. Specifications
V. Standards
VI. Industry/Organizational Documents
VII. Other Documents
VIII. Requirements
IX. General Project Description
X. Detailed Project Requirements
XI. Systems Engineering
XII. Systems Analysis and Control
XIII. Baseline Generation
XIV. Software Design
XV. Hardware Design
XVI. Training Design, Delivery, and Installation
XVII. Concept of Operations
XVIII. Maintenance/Customer Support
XIX. Design Reviews
XX. System Requirements Review
XXI. System Design Review
XXII. Program Management
XXIII. Program Management System
XXIV. Risk Assessment, Mitigation, and Management Program
XXV. Life Cycle Cost Analysis and Control
XXVI. Program Electronic Database
XXVII. Acceptance Criteria
XXVIII. General Guidelines
XXIX. Buyer's Measure of Acceptability
XXX. Product Demonstration Milestones
XXXI. Test/Review Requirements
XXXII. Provider's Responsibility for Demonstrating Product Acceptability
XXXIII. Reporting Requirements
XXXIV. Review Meetings
XXXV. Status Reports

FIGURE 2.2.   Statement of Work Format

The SOW format in Figure 2.2 may be more comprehensive than needed for a specific project, particularly if the project is relatively small and does not have the usual complexities of most projects. If that is the case, use the applicable sections of the format and skip the others. Likewise, add any sections not in the format that are important to the success of the project. Remember that every project is unique, so providing a format that fits every situation is difficult if not impossible.

The focus thus far in this chapter has been primarily from the viewpoint of the customer. Understanding what requirements are, how the customer develops them, and how they are transmitted to the provider is essential to understanding the next step: interpreting an SOW and identifying the requirements.

IDENTIFYING PROJECT REQUIREMENTS

Generally, identifying project requirements is not difficult if the SOW and other project documents are carefully examined. This does not mean that it is a small task, because the task of identifying requirements becomes more difficult as the project size and complexity grow. Even for small projects, vagueness of requirements makes the task formidable. Still, the task need not be difficult if there is a disciplined process in place.

Defense industry companies generally have a well-defined requirements identification processes because their survival is directly dependent upon their ability to successfully bid on and win contracts. Other companies, public or private, that are dependent upon bidding for business also know how to identify and interpret customer requirements. Most other companies and organizations typically have a very difficult time identifying their customers' requirements and often do not even realize the need for it. The process outlined below should help you if your organization does not have a process to identify requirements in place.

Every company may approach requirements identification in a slightly different way, but the basic process is essentially the same regardless of the industry and regardless of whether the customer is internal or external. The steps in this process are:

- Determine whether the project is one that should be pursued
- Look for special conditions stated by the customer

- Capture all the requirements in every document pertaining to the project
- Develop a matrix that cross-references each requirement to where it is found and where it is addressed in the project plan

Although only four steps are listed in this process, each step has multiple substeps. They are addressed in detail in the next several sections.

Determining Whether to Pursue a Project

Many companies assign people or even a department to be responsible for determining whether a project, internal or external, is one that should be pursued. This would seem to be an obvious thing to do, but the fact is, there are just as many companies that do not have any kind of a formal review process and therefore find themselves in the middle of a project that never should have been started.

Bid or project review generally is accomplished by an ad hoc committee constituted specifically for the purpose, which sits in review as the need arises. Figure 2.3 presents a checklist for considering whether to bid on an external solicitation. The checklist is equally applicable, with minor alteration, for determining the viability of pursuing a project that develops within an organization.

The first two checklist questions deal with examining a solicitation or project in light of a company's core business and whether the project will improve the company's market share or meet other corporate goals. Many companies chase contracts or projects that appear achievable or customers offer opportunities the company thinks it knows enough about to satisfy minimal project requirements, believing that these factors provide enough advantage. The company discovers too late that it does not have the requisite expertise and experience or that the project is not a part of its core business. Even if an upcoming project is within the core business, it does not mean the project would further the company's goals. If, for example, a company is targeting projects that provide opportunities to enhance its technical capability, then projects should be under the core business umbrella but with elements that enhance its expertise.

Questions 3, 4, and 5 in Figure 2.3 focus attention on the current internal capability to perform the project. Before embarking on a bid for any contract or before pursuing any project, it is necessary to understand if there are any

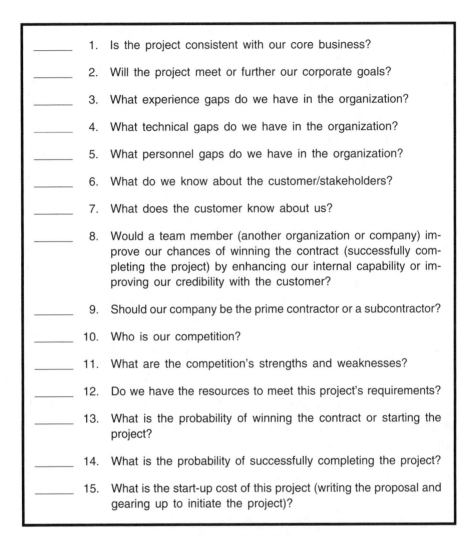

FIGURE 2.3. **Checklist for Making a Bid/No-Bid Decision**

existing gaps in the company's capability to perform. If so, then alternatives need to be developed to allow the company to pursue the project (if the responses to questions 1 and 2 are positive).

Questions 6 and 7 are more difficult to quantify than the previous five questions because they deal with perceptions. A company can be confident that its marketing department has made all possible efforts to get to know a customer and vice versa. However, whether the customer really knows or likes the company remains questionable unless they share previous contracting experience. If the company has not done work for that customer previously, then the question becomes: "Do we have time to educate the customer about us?" Usually the answer to that question is no unless it is known that the project will not be initiated for a least a year and less if the customer is internal to the organization.

Otherwise, questions 8 and 9 of the checklist become very important. Note that these two questions, which deal with the possibility of teaming with one or more companies, support questions 3, 4, and 5 as well. In other words, if there are technical, experiential, or personnel gaps within the company, the chances of a contract win or a successful project improve by teaming with companies or organizations that can fill those gaps. Likewise, teaming with a company that has a long positive history with a customer is one of the best and quickest ways to become known to the customer.

Questions 10 and 11 have to do with accomplishing a competitive analysis. All the likely bidders should be known, along with their relationship to and experience with the customer. If the competitive analysis reveals that the company is likely to be the highest bidder, all the other questions in Figure 2.3 become moot.

Finally, if the answers to all the other questions are positive and the cost of initiating the project is within company guidelines, then the project should be pursued. Otherwise, the project should be avoided regardless of how attractive it appears on the surface.

Once it is decided a project will be pursued, then the serious work of identifying the requirement details begins.

Special Customer Conditions

Almost all projects have specific conditions that have to be met in addition to the usual project/product requirements. Usually, these conditions are easily identified because the customer will draw attention to them even if lax in the description of the project's general requirements. The most common special conditions, some of which are actually constraints, are:

- Schedule
- Reporting cycles and types of information expected
- Budget

- Environmental standards
- Developmental and quality standards
- Exclusions from participating in follow-on contracts

It is not uncommon for the project completion date to be dictated. That is understandable since the project is in place to address a need and usually that need has to be met by or before a specific date. In information technology and other highly competitive industries, there almost always is a window of opportunity for the product to be on the market. If the window of opportunity is missed, then the value of the project is zero or at least greatly diminished.

Many customers, in particular those in the federal sector, dictate the number and types of reports, reviews, inspections, and meetings that they expect. In addition, they specify the kind and depth of information to be presented and the frequency of these events. In the private sector, such requirements exist, but usually they are less stringent and often are left to the provider to determine what, how much, and when to report progress.

The budget earmarked for a project also can be a limiting factor, particularly if the customer has not performed a good estimate of the likely cost to perform the project. It often happens that a project is begun with inadequate funding.

Standards of all types are usually a part of any formal solicitation, and even internal customers provide guidance about how the product will be assessed. In many industries, there are standards imposed by regulating agencies, developmental practices, and financial institutions. All the pertinent standards are listed in a formal solicitation, and they should be identified and listed for an internal project as well.

Occasionally there are specific instructions to the provider that if the project is undertaken, then the company will be barred from performing any follow-on projects that evolve from the given project. An example of such a situation would be a project that is done to determine the requirements and specifications for another project. A company that develops these requirements and specifications would have a decided advantage over any other company if the customer issued a solicitation for the follow-on work. Hence, the customer will usually bar the original provider from bidding so that the competition would be fair. This, however, is not something that happens very often in the private sector and especially not in the information technology industry.

The special conditions or requirements are generally not difficult to spot because, first, they tend to "jump out at you" and, second, they are usually highlighted by the customer. In fact, it is common, if there is formal project documentation, for the customer to include a paragraph with the heading "Special Conditions." But ferreting out all the other requirements can be a challenge unless you follow some simple guidelines.

Capturing All the Project Requirements

Formal Solicitations

If identifying requirements is difficult, it is because one must read every line of every document that is provided about the project. The good news is that 99% of the requirements are contained in the SOW. The problem is that some projects, because of their complexity or because of the sheer size of the effort, have other documents such as specifications, the contract, engineering drawings, and other explanatory material associated with the solicitation.

There are two key things to remember if you are involved in such a project. First, the SOW is the governing document. Any other document is subservient. Thus, if there is a specification attached to the SOW and the specification describes the product's size or function differently than the SOW, contractually the SOW is the guiding document. Of course, the wise project manager will clarify the discrepancy. But don't make the mistake of thinking the specification, because it is a more detailed description of the product, is the correct version. Second, although the SOW is the primary or guiding document when resolving discrepancies, it is not the only document that contains requirements. The requirements search must be carried through-out all existing project documentation.

In a formal solicitation, the requirements search is actually simplified because all requirements are introduced with a "shall" clause. That is, the SOW or other documents will state: "The provider shall build…" or "The product shall be capable of…." Therefore, identifying requirements begins by finding and listing all the "shall" statements. Incidentally, in such formal solicitations if the customer intends to provide equipment, data, special tools, or anything else to support the project, the customer identifies these items by introducing them with a "will" clause. For example: "The buyer will provide to the contractor data to support the…" or "The buyer will provide computers for the…." Thus, it is equally important to identify what the customer brings to the project because that affects how the project is planned and especially how the schedule and costs are estimated.

Internal or Informal Projects

It is far more difficult to determine project requirements for those projects that are internal to an organization than it is for formal solicitations because typically there is little or no documentation describing the product. Early in this chapter, I pointed out that every project should have an SOW describing precisely what is to be accomplished in the effort. However, the general feeling is that if a project is internal to an organization, there is no need for a formal SOW. There is no need for an SOW as formal as is found in a solicitation, but at a minimum there needs to be a scope statement describing the product, the customer's requirements, special items such as schedule and budget, and the criteria for project completion.

Once all the requirements are identified and listed, then the most important step in the process occurs: developing a cross-referencing matrix.

Cross-Referencing Requirements Matrix

The cross-referencing requirements matrix is a useful tool for mapping the requirements against where they are found (i.e., in the SOW, specifications, drawings, and so on) and against where they are addressed in the work breakdown structure. Figure 2.4 is a sample of a requirements matrix to demonstrate how this tool is developed. Note that it is only a partial matrix for a fictitious project. A complete matrix can be several pages long.

This matrix serves several useful purposes for the project manager. First, it serves as a worksheet for identifying the requirements. Just having the form in front of you helps you focus on the task of identifying all the requirements, and in this capacity it is a constant reminder that requirements exist in all relevant project documents. Second, many of the same requirements will be addressed in different documents. Hence, the cross-referencing action allows the project team to determine not only which documents discuss the same requirement but also whether the description in each is the same. If it is not, then the customer needs to be notified and asked for clarification. Remember, though, that until or unless the inconsistency is clarified, the SOW is the guiding document. Third, the cross-referencing document provides a way of ensuring that each requirement is

Requirements	Statement of Work	Spec	Drawing	Work Breakdown Structure
Provide a distributed IT infrastructure for the AJAX project	Para 1, Scope Definition	Intro	Drawing 1	2.3.2 Dist. IT Infrastructure
Develop a grid communication system to support AJAX	Para 6.b, Section C		Drawing 3	2.3.2.1 Design & Model Grid Architecture
Integrate all AJAX software services	Para 3.c, Section E			2.3.2.2 Integrate Software Services
Develop a data management system	Para 14 & 15, Section G		Drawings 6, 7	2.3.3 Grid Data Management
Integrate database tools to management ultralarge databases	Para 4.g.2, Section B			2.3.3.1 Integrate Database Tools
Develop, integrate, test tools and middle-ware infrastructure to support and manage petabyte-scale information volumes		Para 13		2.3.3.2 Build Middleware Infrastructure

FIGURE 2.4. Sample Cross-Referencing Requirements Matrix

addressed in the work breakdown structure. If it is not in the work breakdown structure, then it is not in the project.

Identifying requirements should not be drudgery. It is not difficult, but it does require attention to detail and it requires that every document initiating the project be thoroughly reviewed. Unless all the requirements are identified before the planning begins, then the project can suffer delays, additional costs, and even failure.

SUMMARY

Requirements are the reasons for projects. The customer has a need to be satisfied and provides the project team with requirements to satisfy that need. It is the function of the project manager and the project team to correctly identify all requirements of the project and to provide a plan that, when implemented, will satisfy each of the requirements.

The most important document that customers use to transmit requirements is the SOW. An SOW is always provided for a formal solicitation, but not usually for an internal project. However, organizations need to make the SOW a part of their operating policies. Lacking that, when a project manager is assigned a project, he or she should prepare an SOW, as he or she understands the project scope, and get the customer's endorsement before the project is initiated.

Identifying requirements is not difficult when well-written project documentation is available. It does, however, require attention to detail and a thorough review of all the documentation. An important and very useful tool in identifying all the project requirements is the cross-referencing matrix. This matrix not only helps identify the requirements but also provides a way to reference each requirement to each relevant project document and to determine if the descriptions are consistent if a requirement is referred to in more than one document. Finally, and perhaps the most important function of this matrix, each requirement can be referenced to the work breakdown structure to ensure that it is specifically addressed in the project plan.

Poorly written or misinterpreted requirements are the biggest cause of project failure. Properly identifying the customer's requirements, whether the customer is external or internal to the organization, and developing and executing a strong project plan to address these requirements is the major function of the project manager and his or her team.

3

WORK BREAKDOWN STRUCTURE AND BASELINE DEVELOPMENT

A work breakdown structure (WBS) is essentially the scope statement reduced to individual pieces of work. The *PMBOK® Guide* defines the WBS as *a deliverable-oriented grouping of project elements that organizes and defines the total work scope of the project. Each descending level represents an increasingly detailed definition of the project work.* This definition might be misleading to some because it implies that a WBS can be defined only by deliverables, which is fine as long as it is understood that a deliverable extends to the task level. In other words, deliverable means more than the finished contracted product or products; it includes all those tasks that lead to the finished product.

A better definition for WBS may be: *a task-oriented grouping of project elements that organizes and defines the total work scope of the project. It is a structured way of breaking down a project into work packages.* Either way, the objective is to develop the WBS starting with the highest level and least amount of detail (for example, build a Web site) and progressively break the project scope into the individual pieces that make up the whole (for example, test the functionality of the completed Web site). The hierarchical organization, in which larger elements are broken down into smaller ones, is the key to the WBS. It is not just a random to-do list.

BENEFITS AND USES OF A WORK BREAKDOWN STRUCTURE

The WBS is the most important project management tool because it completely identifies all the work that is described by the project scope and provides the basis for detailed project planning, control, and implementation. It protects the project manager from the "gold-plating" that can occur as a project moves along by preventing the application of time and resources to work that should not be done. The WBS is also the basis for every other tool the project manager develops and uses to plan, implement, and control the project. The WBS itself is not a schedule or cost estimate, but it provides the underlying framework for developing both of these key management tools. It can be a crucial tool for purposes of communication, particularly when negotiating for resources or when discussing scope changes to the project. In short, the WBS is a structured way of decomposing a project into its various components: hardware, software, services, documentation, labor, testing, delivery, and installation. It is a formalized way of reducing the project into successively lower levels of greater detail.

As a multipurpose tool, some important uses of the WBS are as a basis for assigning task responsibility, project costing, network analysis, scheduling, and project control.

Assigning Task Responsibility

Assigning task responsibility is one of the most important uses of the WBS. The completed WBS will expose all the component parts of the project down to a workable level of detail. Once this is done, it will be self-evident who should do each piece of work and who should supervise each effort. The project manager, in coordination with the appropriate functional managers, will develop a task responsibility matrix, assigning a name to each of the WBS elements. This task responsibility matrix then shows at a glance who is responsible for every piece of work on the project.

Project Costing

The second most important use of the WBS is project costing. It is virtually impossible to estimate the cost of a project by viewing the project as a whole.

Clearly, a project has to be reduced to smaller elements until the cost of each element can be determined. As the cost of each smaller element is determined, the costs are "rolled up," to finally obtain one number for the whole project. The WBS is the perfect tool for this purpose since it decomposes the project into sufficient detail that the cost of each element can be determined. Figure 3.1 shows a sample WBS.

It is crucial to include the project management function as a separate line-item entry in the WBS. Every other entry includes the labor cost of the tasks, but the project manager and any other project office staff spread their labor costs across the entire project. That is, the project manager does not

```
1.0  Management Information Software System
     1.1  Gap Analysis
          1.1.1  Needs Assessment
                 1.1.1.1  Measure State of Current System
                 1.1.1.2  Determine Additional Capability Requirements
          1.1.2  Develop Alternative Approaches
     1.2  Requirements Specification
          1.2.1  Develop Preliminary Software Specifications
          1.2.2  Develop Detailed Software Specifications
          1.2.3  Develop Preliminary Hardware Specifications
     1.3  Systems Engineering
          1.3.1  Develop Alternative Software Approaches
          1.3.2  Develop Alternative Hardware Approaches
          1.3.3  Develop Cost Estimates for Each Alternative Approach
          1.3.4  Determine Best Technical and Most Cost-Effective Approach
          1.3.5  Develop Preferred System Architecture
     1.4  System Design
          1.4.1  Develop Preliminary System Design
                 1.4.1.1  Design Software Modules
                 1.4.1.2  Design Hardware Subsystems
                 1.4.1.3  Integrate Systems
                 1.4.1.4  Develop Detailed System Design
     1.5  System Development
          1.5.1  Write Code for System Modules
          1.5.2  Construct Hardware Subsystems
          1.5.3  Develop Prototype
```

FIGURE 3.1. Sample Work Breakdown Structure

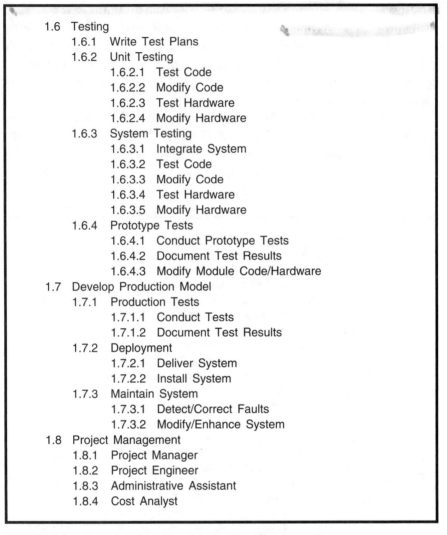

1.6 Testing
  1.6.1 Write Test Plans
  1.6.2 Unit Testing
      1.6.2.1 Test Code
      1.6.2.2 Modify Code
      1.6.2.3 Test Hardware
      1.6.2.4 Modify Hardware
  1.6.3 System Testing
      1.6.3.1 Integrate System
      1.6.3.2 Test Code
      1.6.3.3 Modify Code
      1.6.3.4 Test Hardware
      1.6.3.5 Modify Hardware
  1.6.4 Prototype Tests
      1.6.4.1 Conduct Prototype Tests
      1.6.4.2 Document Test Results
      1.6.4.3 Modify Module Code/Hardware
1.7 Develop Production Model
  1.7.1 Production Tests
      1.7.1.1 Conduct Tests
      1.7.1.2 Document Test Results
  1.7.2 Deployment
      1.7.2.1 Deliver System
      1.7.2.2 Install System
  1.7.3 Maintain System
      1.7.3.1 Detect/Correct Faults
      1.7.3.2 Modify/Enhance System
1.8 Project Management
  1.8.1 Project Manager
  1.8.2 Project Engineer
  1.8.3 Administrative Assistant
  1.8.4 Cost Analyst

FIGURE 3.1. Sample Work Breakdown Structure (continued)

just work on a task. He or she is supervising the entire project. Therefore, rather than try to apportion the project manager's time to every single task, it is much easier to include a separate WBS entry for this function and then provide a total cost for the estimated project duration. Otherwise, it is impossible to capture all the project staff costs.

Network Analysis

The WBS provides the basis for development of the network analysis, a method of representing the activities or tasks of a project by a series of lines and nodes to show the interrelations of these various activities. Several important pieces of information can be derived from a network analysis: the critical path, which is the path that takes the longest to traverse (the critical path determines the minimum schedule length with a given resource allocation), early start and finish times for each activity, and the amount of slack time the project manager can expect for each activity. See Chapter 4 for a discussion of how to develop and interpret a network.

Scheduling

Scheduling the project activities is difficult unless there is a clear understanding of all the activity requirements and how each of the activities relates to one another. For instance, suppose a number of activities cannot begin until one or more preceding activities have been completed. Without a detailed breakdown of the project, it is easy to overlook these interrelationships or to overlook certain activities completely. The WBS, then, is a way to analyze a project's activities from the perspective of creating schedules, each of which will have the requisite beginning and ending points, while observing their dependency hierarchies.

Project Control

Controlling a project requires a complete understanding of the project activities: who is responsible for each, how they interrelate, how much each element should cost, and how long each activity should take to complete. The WBS is the basis for each of the tools already discussed, which in turn are the tools that the project manager uses to track and control a project.

WORK BREAKDOWN STRUCTURE MODELS

The WBS can take multiple forms. The two most common forms are the indented WBS and the graphic WBS. The same information can be displayed in either format, and both can be used on the same project. Excerpts from a WBS for a project intended to update the management information system capability for an organization are shown in Figure 3.2, which depicts the WBS in the graphic format. Figure 3.3 shows the same project segment in the indented WBS format.

The graphic WBS format more easily shows the relative levels of the work to be accomplished and works well as a communication tool. It clearly shows vertical integration of segments from smaller to larger components of the project scope. It can provide a very effective briefing slide and can be easily adjusted to the levels of detail that are appropriate for different audiences. Two major disadvantages of the graphic format are that the graphic becomes

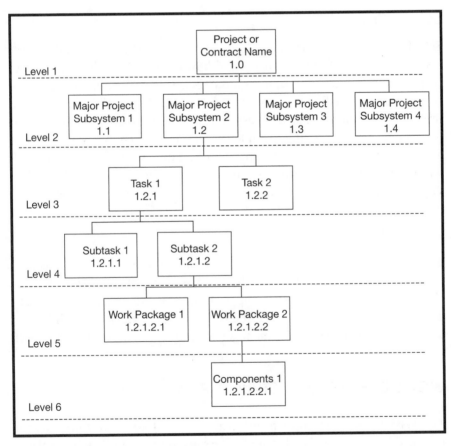

FIGURE 3.2.   Graphic Work Breakdown Structure Format

WBS Number	Description	WBS Level
1.0 Project or Contract Name		1
1.1 Major Project Subdivision		2
1.1.1 Task		3
1.1.1.1 Subtask		4
1.1.1.1.1 Work Package		5
1.1.1.1.1.1 Components		6

FIGURE 3.3. Indented Work Breakdown Structure Format

very large for complex projects and, second, most project management software packages do not automatically provide this WBS format.

The indented WBS format has different advantages. It is easier to include a greater level of detail. It is also the way that scope breakdowns are loaded into major software tools, and that allows for easy editing, printing, and computerized monitoring. In other words, all project management software packages automatically display this format and adjust it when changes are made.

It is best to be able to use either approach, depending on the purpose and the audience. Some people interpret information more easily when they see it graphically; others prefer lists. What works best for a particular project depends on the project team and the customer's needs. The best approach might be to use a highly detailed indented format to guide the team in performing its work and a less detailed graphic diagram to brief senior management or the client.

The wording used in the WBS deserves some consideration. Some people prefer entries to be nouns that state the work output (for example, "user interface" or "performance test"). This works best for projects with mostly clear, discrete outputs. It is the style that seems to be suggested by the emphasis in the *PMBOK® Guide* on the WBS being deliverable oriented. Often, though, particularly in service-oriented projects, subject-verb wording better describes the work (for example, "develop user interface" or "perform system test"). Either style is acceptable. The important thing is to select the one that best fits the organization's guidance and is easiest for the project team to understand.

BUILDING A WORK BREAKDOWN STRUCTURE

The WBS can also be organized around project products or by phases. The most important point is not the format chosen but the inclusion of all the work in the WBS regardless of the method of displaying it.

The most effective approach to developing the WBS is from the top down, that is, by breaking the whole project into progressively smaller pieces. This process begins with an understanding of the purpose of the project. Based on that understanding, the project is broken down into its major segments of work. Then the major segments are broken down into their component parts, and each component is further decomposed into its sub-components. This process continues until a level of detail that is sufficient for assigning and monitoring project work is attained. This is known as the top-down approach to building a WBS.

The lowest WBS level is called the *work package* level. It is the level at which the project manager can assign resources and track progress, without getting bogged down in too much detail. How big or how small should a work package be? There is no hard and fast answer, but one good guideline is to be sure that each work package is small enough to assign to an individual or small team. Another is that no work package should exceed 80 hours of work—the 80-hour rule. The 80-hour rule is used by the Project Management Institute as a rule of thumb to help define work package size, but, clearly, many tasks require longer than 80 hours to complete. In those cases, it is best to assign discrete milestones to the task to artificially break it into segments that are easier to monitor and control. If, on the other hand, while working on plans for costs, schedules, and resources, there is a need to consider part of a work package in one place and another part later or someplace else, it is probably more than one work package and requires reexamination to correctly identify the work.

Every activity required by the scope statement must be covered in a work package, sometimes also referred to as a *task* or an *activity*. If something is not in a work package, it should not be done. Obviously, there are individual components and work efforts that are at lower levels than the work package, but these should not be separated in the WBS. Much of this sort of information should go into the WBS dictionary, which is discussed next. The important point is that if a work package is too small, it will be micromanaged, and if it is too large, project monitoring and control will be difficult.

Control account is a term that is used in a project management sense, not in a purely accounting sense. In project management, it means the level at which costs are tracked for project and senior managers and for more general monitoring without too much detail. Typically, the control account is one level above the work packages, but this approach may vary. Because different sections of a WBS will have different levels, and some sections will be followed more carefully by senior managers than others, the project manager will have to carefully determine what level to use to control and report on the project rather than follow some specific numeric rule.

In addition to the top-down approach to building a WBS, there is a bottom-up approach. In this approach, team members brainstorm and identify as many activities as possible. Then the activities are organized into their logical task groups. Task groups are then organized into phases or major components. After organizing this preliminary WBS, the project manager should question the team about how to perform the project better. For example, what testing activities can be developed, and how can defects be identified and corrected? The project manager should make sure such questions are answered before the WBS is finalized.

As an example, consider building a WBS for the development of a Web site from the bottom up. The first step would be to ask team members to list detailed tasks they think would need to be performed to create a Web site. After listing the tasks, the team members group the tasks into categories. For example, a business analyst on the team might know how to define user requirements for the Web site. A systems analyst might know the hardware and software requirements. The team then groups these varied requirements into one broader category called *identify requirements.* The same approach would be followed until all the work-package-level components have been identified and incorporated into groupings of major work segments.

Work Breakdown Structure Dictionary

The WBS dictionary is the way to capture essential information about each work package without cluttering up the WBS. The dictionary documents the information necessary to actually carry out each work package. It ensures that all critical information about an activity is captured and made clear to each team member, including who is responsible for completing the activity, what input is required, and what needs to happen before and after. The WBS dictionary is extremely helpful when bringing new people into the project because it clearly says what is expected in a particular piece of work.

Dictionary items for a two-day work package called *identify business requirements* might include the following:

- **Resources**—Business case, project charter, end users, other stake-holders, project manager, business analyst, systems analyst, facilitator, facilitation meeting room
- **Deliverables**—Requirements specification
- **Predecessors**—Identify project scope, identify stakeholders
- **Successors**—Obtain client approval of business requirements
- **Description**—The project manager, business analyst, and systems analyst organize and conduct a facilitated workshop, run by an independent facilitator, to gather customer business requirements

A sample WBS dictionary form is shown in Figure 3.4.

WHERE DOES THE WORK BREAKDOWN STRUCTURE ORIGINATE?

Not every WBS needs to be developed from scratch. A variety of templates are available through popular software tools. Project managers may look for guidance from past projects. Internally, they can turn to other project managers or to documentation repositories. Externally, they can look for help from industry publications.

But project managers cannot just rely on what already exists. Their creative energy and that of the project leadership team will be needed to construct a WBS, especially when dealing with first-time projects or projects done in a completely new environment. Under no circumstances should anyone expect to pull a WBS off the shelf and use it without adjustments. Remember that, by definition, no two projects are ever exactly alike; at a minimum, projects will be different because different team members are involved. To a large degree, the WBS format and documented use are dependent upon the organizational structure. Figure 3.5 shows the typical WBS to organization relationship.

WORK BREAKDOWN STRUCTURE DICTIONARY

FISCAL YEAR	
2007	
2008	

THIS TASK IS	
RECURRING	
NONRECURRING	

WBS ELEMENT NO.

RFP NUMBER	
PERSON RESPONSIBLE	

WBS ELEMENT NO.

Attach Supporting Documentation
to Show Estimating Rationale

WBS ELEMENT NO.

WORK SCHEDULE

WBS HOURS AND COST

PERSON RESPONSIBLE	LABOR CAT.	FROM	TO	LABOR HOURS	ODC	MATERIAL COST	TOTAL
						WBS ELEMENT COST	

FIGURE 3.4.   Sample Work Breakdown Structure Dictionary

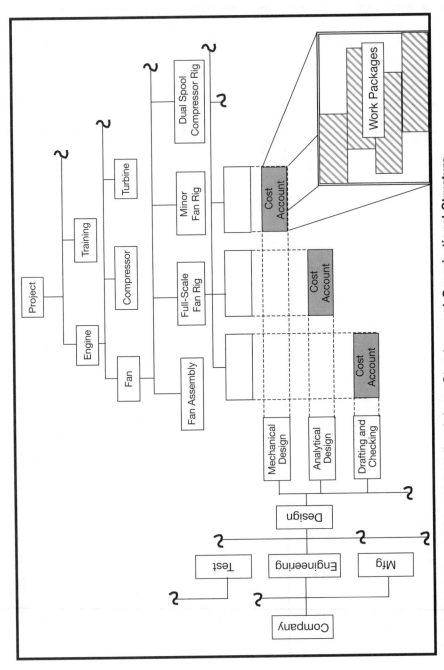

FIGURE 3.5.   Integration of Work Breakdown Structure and Organizational Structure

TRANSLATING THE WORK BREAKDOWN STRUCTURE INTO THE PLAN

The primary purpose of the WBS is to identify all the work within the project scope, but in order to plan how the project will be executed, work must be quantified, not just identified. What the WBS identifies must be quantified before planning can continue. In the WBS, the project scope is broken down into small assignable units called work packages. These work packages must be planned specifically and integrated together into the project plan.

Integrating those packages requires information about the work packages beyond the definition of the work itself. It is important to know how long each package will take to perform, how much it will cost, the resources it will require, and so on. This is the role of estimating. Planning cannot go forward without these estimates.

The more estimating is treated as a deliberate process and not just guessing, the more likely success is to follow. The basic concepts of estimating apply to all aspects of estimating. In other words, gathering data to estimate time follows the same basic process as gathering data to estimate cost. Figure 3.6 shows the estimating process.

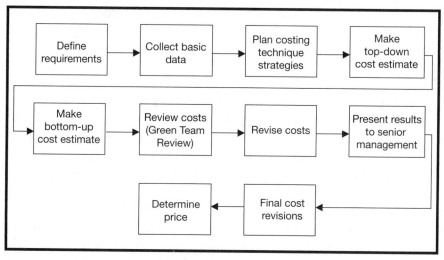

FIGURE 3.6.   Estimating Process Steps

THE BASELINE

Everyone understands the general concept of a "baseline"; it is a starting point. What many people do not understand is what a project baseline is, when and if it can be changed, the components of a baseline, and how it is used to control the progress of a project.

This section defines baseline and its various components. It also discusses how to determine these various baseline components using some fundamental estimating processes or techniques, how to interpret data gained from time-phased distributions of the project cost information, and then how to establish the baseline for a project. What many project managers do not understand is that there actually are three baselines that collectively define the overall project baseline. This section discusses all these issues in some detail.

The baseline is critical to project success because it establishes the expectations of both the customer and all other stakeholders. In short, it is model against which the project will be conducted and the deliverables will be built. The baseline, as given in *Project Management Terms: A Working Glossary* by LeRoy Ward, is defined as:

1. Original plan (for a project, work package, or activity), plus or minus any approved changes. May be used with a modifier (for example, cost baseline, schedule baseline, performance measurement baseline).
2. Nominal plan to which deviations will be compared.

The first definition is important because it implies that there is more than one baseline—and that is true. Hence, there can be some confusion here because the very word "baseline" connotes a singular starting place. Actually, the definition is meant to show that the overall project baseline has embedded in it three distinct but intricately related baselines: the schedule, the cost, and the technical. Together these comprise the performance measurement baseline.

It is important to note that a baseline represents the WBS and any approved changes. In other words, it is what the project is all about and how it is going to be accomplished, and both the customer and the key stakeholders approve it. Once the baseline is established, it is changed only through a formal process, and the customer and key stakeholders must approve the changes.

Technical Baseline

The technical baseline is in many ways the most crucial of the three because it describes the "what" of the project, that is, the deliverable(s). It is very important to establish buy-in from the customer that what is described in the plan is actually what the customer wants; this buy-in or sign-off is obviously critical. Just as critical is buy-in from the organizational stakeholders because they have to support the effort and, in most cases, provide the resources and technical expertise to make it happen.

The problem is that project managers and team members seldom are involved in the early definition of the technical baseline; marketing or business development personnel in conjunction with the customer often define the technical baseline before it ever becomes a project. It falls to the project manager to provide the details of the technical problem and to determine whether the organization even has the expertise or resource capability to accomplish it. That is why this baseline becomes so important, and it is why the project manager must define it *completely* and get final buy-in from both the customer and the other stakeholders.

Cost Baseline

The cost baseline is derived from the estimates of the work to be done. It is usually shown as a cumulative estimated cost or budget curve of all the tasks and associated support— including people—that are expected to be needed during the life cycle of a project. The cost estimates are determined from the WBS and in conjunction with schedule development. Many practitioners contend that costs are first determined and then schedules built to support the costs; others hold that the schedules are first determined and then the costs. The fact is, costs and schedules are best determined together because almost all organizations have to optimize their resources, which requires some subtle and sometimes not-so-subtle shifting and sharing of resources from one project to another. This of necessity means that resources and schedules have to be played against each other to obtain the most efficient and cost-effective baselines possible.

Having said all that, the cost estimate is begun by decomposing the WBS to the work package level and assigning resources to each work package and then determining the cost and the duration for the work. Every work package is approached in this way, and the overall cost of the project is determined by rolling up the individual work package cost from the bottom to the top of the WBS. Once the overall costs are determined, then the process of optimizing them by changing resources and durations of individual work packages to arrive at the most optimum and practical budget and schedule can begin.

Cost Baseline Components

The cost baseline, unlike the schedule baseline, has several important components that need to be understood by the project manager because each of these components is used in different ways, and in some cases not by the project manager at all. In contract work, the use of these components has a legal aspect that can cause serious problems for the organization if they are not used in accordance with standard accounting practices or in accordance with federal guidelines. Generally, this is not too much of a problem for the project manager, but it behooves him or her to know how the cost baseline is developed using its various components. The different cost components are discussed in detail in Chapter 5.

Schedule Baseline

The schedule baseline is developed in the same general fashion as the cost baseline. That is, the WBS is developed to the work package level and durations estimated for each work package. A network analysis is developed next to show the interdependencies of each task so that a reasoned decision can be made regarding the viability of pursuing the project as it is currently structured. Whether an adjustment to the sequence of task work is required is a function of whether one or more of the tasks could actually be done in parallel or if they absolutely must follow sequentially, whether the planned task work conflicts with other projects in the organization, and whether the expertise exists to do some of the work at all. All these factors are considered in the development of the duration of each task. Furthermore, the skill level and experience of the resources for each task have to be considered in the duration estimate; clearly, highly skilled and experienced people can accomplish the work sooner than those not so skilled and experienced, but it could cost more.

Performance Measurement Baseline

The performance measurement baseline is made up of the other three baselines, but the costs have been collected relative to decisions made about the technical approach and the schedule for accomplishing the technical baseline. These costs are divided into two categories for accounting and tracking convenience. The active account is called distributed budget, and the inactive account is called undistributed budget.

- **Distributed budget**—Those accounts that are used for the open work packages, that is, the work packages that have active work being done. Using the distributed budget category allows the project manager to quickly and easily track the actual expenditures against the planned expenditures for the active tasks.
- **Undistributed budget**—The budget reserved for those tasks that have not begun. Tasks for which work will be done in the future are covered by this budget, and the reason is that, in the accounting context, any open account number or budget technically can be charged against. Having these tasks in an undistributed and unopened category prevents an unexpected use of the funds that have been set aside specifically for these tasks.

Collectively, these three "baselines"—technical, cost, and schedule—comprise the project or scope baseline, which should not be changed except by the customer through a formal contract modification. Once the baseline is established, project planning can begin in earnest.

SUMMARY

technical
cost } *Scope baseline*
schedule

A WBS is essentially the scope statement decomposed into individual pieces of work. The WBS itself is a multipurpose tool from which all other project management tools can be developed—it is the network diagram that leads to project schedules, cost estimates, resource requirements, personnel skill set requirements, and ultimately the project plans. The WBS is also the first document that indicates potential risks in the project.

There are two WBS formats. The indented form, which allows for a greater level of detail, is the way that scope breakdowns are loaded into major software tools, and that allows for easy editing, printing, and computerized monitoring. The graphic format, on the other hand, more clearly shows the levels of the WBS and is a great communication tool.

The WBS dictionary describes the task scope. It tells the task leader what has to be done and the estimated schedule and cost of the task and provides the project manager with a management tool for tracking individual task work.

The baseline is the original plan for the project plus or minus any changes. The project or scope baseline is composed of three individual baselines: the schedule, budget, and performance baselines. Once the baseline is set, it can only be changed by the customer and should never be changed without a formal contract modification.

Two budgetary terms important to the project manager and team are the distributed budget and the undistributed budget. The distributed budget is the active budget being used for project costs; the undistributed budget is the inactive budget that consists of dollars not yet committed or released to the project.

Once the baseline has been established, the next step for the project manager is to develop the project and ancillary plans.

4

SCHEDULING

Scheduling a project requires both a scientific and an artistic touch. It requires a scientific touch because the schedule has to reflect the work breakdown structure tasks (i.e., project requirements) in a logical and interrelated way to optimize resources across the organization. Scheduling requires an artistic touch because tasks not only are technically dependent or interrelated but are often politically driven, thus requiring finesse and interpersonal skill.

Of all the activities in project management, scheduling is the most potent in terms of impact on the project as a whole. Consider that the schedule is developed so that it reflects not only when a task is accomplished relative to all other tasks but also reflects when the appropriate resources are planned for the work, all of which puts in place a mechanism for developing the project costs. Some project managers argue that one should start with the budget and then develop a schedule to fit it. In reality, project managers must determine how long it will take to accomplish the project requirements—given available resources—and then estimate the costs. Any change to the schedule—after it is set—has a profound effect on resource allocation and costs, not to mention the impact on obligations to the customer in terms of delivering on time.

Too many project teams fail to understand the significance of developing schedules that optimize all these important project components; they just put together schedules that fit within the customer's time frame. This chapter discusses the tools of scheduling and the considerations necessary for optimizing schedules.

KEY STEPS IN DEVELOPING SCHEDULES

Data to develop accurate and workable schedules come from a variety of places, and unfortunately, many project teams only focus on one source: the scope statement or customer-established time of delivery. Since there are other key sources of data, they all should be used in every schedule development activity.

INPUT TO ACTIVITY DEFINITION FOR DEVELOPING SCHEDULES

There are several typical sources for obtaining activity or deliverable information. The most common ones are described below. The wise project manager will use as many of these sources as possible.

Scope Statement

The scope statement contains information about the project deliverables and usually contains assumptions and constraints as well. The scope statement or accompanying documents such as contracts, specifications, and drawings also provide important information that affects the schedule.

Work Breakdown Structure

The work breakdown structure (WBS) identifies every task in a project. If something is not in the WBS, then it is not in the project, so make sure every requirement is identified and described in the WBS.

Historical Information

Historical information is information about other similar projects and collected metrics that are useful in refining estimating techniques. This historical information should be collected in the lessons learned files of each project.

Constraints and Assumptions

Constraints and assumptions provide a guide for the limits or educated guesses that are used to form the schedule structure. Constraints usually are in the form of either specifications and customer-imposed delivery dates or they can be due to limited resource and technology capability in the organization. Assumptions are best guesses made when precise data are not available. All constraints and assumptions need to be documented and regularly validated.

Expert Judgments

Expert judgments provide an experienced and objective opinion about some or all of the above data and their sources. Not every organization can afford the expense or the time to hire experts from outside the company, but many companies have resident experts whose experience is seldom tapped. When a draft schedule is developed, senior functional technical and managerial personnel should be asked to review it and offer comments and recommendations. They should be provided with the data sources used, an estimate of the data accuracy, constraints and assumptions, and the objectives of the project so that it is clear how the schedule(s) is to be developed.

NETWORK ANALYSIS

The basis for the schedule is the WBS because it contains all the tasks to be accomplished in a project. The first step in developing the schedule is to develop a network layout or diagram of the WBS work packages, because the network shows the interrelationships of the project tasks. Figure 4.1 shows the relationship between the WBS and the network diagram.

There are some key points that need to be made about the fundamentals of network development and what elements of the WBS are needed to construct the network. The tasks in the network are the *work packages* of the WBS. The term work packages is emphasized because the network must be constructed from the lowest levels of the WBS, not the summary levels, because it would not be possible to identify specific or potential problem areas in a project (i.e., risk points) due to allocated resources if the network only contained the higher level summary activities. All the WBS tasks must be included in the network because they have to be accounted for in the schedule. Leaving even one task out of the network could change the overall schedule duration, estimated costs, and resource allocation commitments.

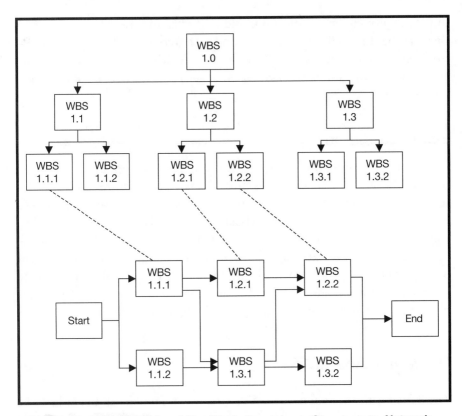

FIGURE 4.1. Relationship of the Work Breakdown Structure to Network Diagram

The WBS is not a schedule, but it is the *basis* for it; the network diagram is a schedule but is used primarily to identify key scheduling information that ultimately goes into user-friendlier schedule formats, such as milestone and Gantt charts.

Interpreting and Using Network Diagrams

The network diagram provides important information to the project team. It provides information about how the tasks are related (i.e., whether they can or need to be accomplished sequentially or in parallel), where risk points are in the schedule, how long it will take as currently planned to finish the project, and when each task needs to begin and end.

Validating the Time Frame

One of the key benefits of the network diagram is that it immediately shows the shortest duration within which project work can be finished. Bear in mind that at least the first time the network diagram is developed, it will be based on assumptions about resource availability, estimated durations of tasks, and judgments about whether tasks are dependent upon each other in a sequential hierarchy or some tasks are independent and can be accomplished in parallel (i.e., at the same time). Some or all of these assumptions may have to be reassessed once the network analysis reveals the total project duration. For example, if the customer dictates a specific due date and the network analysis indicates a longer schedule is required, then all the assumptions used to build the network diagram have to be reassessed to determine if some of the tasks can be done in parallel rather than sequentially, if more resources are needed, if the task duration estimates are correct, and if there is a need to renegotiate the scope.

Considering Risk in Schedule Estimates

Risk should be considered as early in a project as possible. The first time potential risk events become visible is during the development of the WBS because the tasks are described and resource needs begin to emerge. The first time the project manager can see potential risk events and risk points is during the development of the network diagram. The network diagram shows task interdependencies. Hence, the timing for allocating resources is apparent. Knowing when resources are needed for each project allows the balancing of available resources for all projects across the organization.

One crucial risk point occurs when network paths converge. Wherever two or more network paths come together, the risk of schedule slippage occurs because if any of the tasks do not complete on time and converge as originally planned, then all subsequent tasks will be late.

The network diagram provides an opportunity to identify risks early and to incorporate contingencies in the form of time or money. Contingency should be shown in the network diagram as a task so that it is accorded the same importance and managed the same as any task is. Just as task characteristics change over the life of a project, so will the characteristics of the contingency reserves change. Therefore, it is important to reduce or eliminate these reserves as the risk events do or do not materialize.

Whenever risk is identified in the network diagram, it should be documented and a strategy developed to deal with it. One other important aspect about a network diagram is that it can help in the evaluation of the seriousness of a risk. If one considers where in the schedule a risk event is likely to occur, then a more realistic assessment of its seriousness can be made. Even a high-risk event with a significant impact may be considered a low risk if there is sufficient schedule duration remaining to deal with the risk event. However, a low-probability, low-impact risk event that occurs during the final month of a project may be a high risk to the project simply because of time available to deal with the risk consequences. Therefore, consider the percentage of schedule expended and remaining when determining the risk impact.

Knowing generally what a network diagram is and its uses and benefits, it is time to learn how it is actually developed.

NETWORK DIAGRAM DEVELOPMENT

Generally, network diagrams are not difficult to develop if some fundamental rules of thumb are followed. It is important to note here that many new or inexperienced project managers assume they will use a project management software package to create networks diagrams, and it is true that the software can do that. But unless one understands how network diagrams are developed—and the key characteristics of them, it is not possible to look at one and determine whether it is correct. In addition, software packages do not alert the user if he or she makes an error linking, or showing dependencies among, the tasks in the network.

Network Diagram Rules of Thumb

Follow these simple tips to immediately begin developing and analyzing network diagrams:

- **There is a starting and ending point for each network**—This is stating the obvious, but one of the most frequently missed items, especially when using software programs to develop networks, is either starting or ending the network at a definite point. The starting or ending point can be a WBS task, provided the entire network emanates from a single task and ends at a single task. Generally, however, it is best to create a specific start and end point, or an empty node, for the network.

- **There are predecessors and successors for all tasks**—From the starting point until the end point, each task will have tasks or events before it (predecessors) and each task will have tasks or events after it (successors). In other words, every task must be connected to some other task or event; otherwise a task is left hanging in space and the network analysis cannot be completed accurately. Again, project management software packages do not warn that there is an error in the network development, so the result can provide incorrect schedule information.
- **The network must be updated and current**—Just as the project plan is a dynamic plan, so is the network dynamic—it changes. Also, the network logic (that is, the placing of the tasks relative to each other) must be constantly reviewed and updated because the logic ultimately defines when each task begins and ends.
- **There are no loops**—Every task must be connected to some other task(s) or event(s), but be careful that the connections do not result in a loop (i.e., a path that closes on itself).

Before the advent of computer software to help with network diagram generation, network diagrams were rarely updated because they were so cumbersome and difficult to develop. With software as a tool, however, a network diagrams can be updated quickly and often with little work.

NETWORK DIAGRAM TYPES

There are many types of network diagrams, but the two classic ones are the activity on arrow (AOA) and the activity on node (AON). The latter is now the one most commonly used and is supported by all project management programs.

PERT (project or program evaluation research technique) is the best-known AOA-type diagram and is the historical basis of all network diagramming. It was developed in the 1950s for the Department of the Navy to aid in monitoring and tracking the very large, very complex Polaris program. AON is what is commonly referred to as the precedence diagramming method

AON = activity on node
precedence diagramming method -

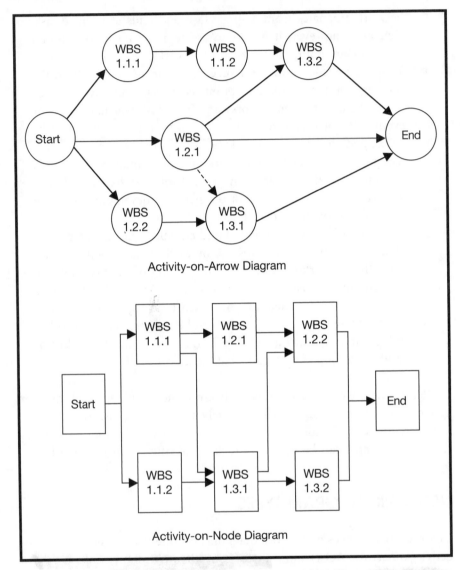

FIGURE 4.2.   Examples of the Activity-on-Arrow and Activity-on-Node Diagrams

(PDM). Microsoft Project, for example, uses the PDM as its network view, in spite of the fact that older versions of the software referred to it as PERT. Figure 4.2 shows these two types of networks, with the AOA network at the top of the graphic and the AON at the bottom.

There are some major differences between and advantages and disadvantages to the AOA and AON diagrams that should be understood.

Activity-on-Arrow Networks   *arrows = activities/tasks*

The AOA diagram is traditionally drawn using circles as the nodes, with nodes representing the beginning and ending points of the arrows or tasks. In the AOA network, the arrows represent the activities or tasks. All network diagrams have the advantages already mentioned, such as showing task interdependencies, start and end times, and the critical path (the shortest path through the network), but the AOA network also has some disadvantages that limit the use of the method. The three major disadvantages of the AOA method are:

- The AOA network can only show finish-to-start relationships. It simply is not possible to show lead and lag except by adding or subtracting time, which makes project tracking difficult if not impossible.
- There are instances when "dummy" activities can occur in an AOA network. Dummy activities are activities that show the dependency of one task on other tasks but for other than technical reasons. For example, a task may be dependent on another because it would be more cost effective to use the same resources for the two; otherwise, the two tasks could be accomplished in parallel. Dummy activities do not have durations associated with them; they simply show that a task has some kind of dependence on another task.
- AOA diagrams are not as widely used as AON simply because the latter are somewhat simpler to use and all project management software programs can accommodate AON networks, whereas not all can accommodate AOA networks.

Activity-on-Node Networks

As the name implies, in AON or precedence diagramming, the nodes indicate the activities or tasks. In this case, the arrows simply show dependencies.

The PDM has some advantages over the AOA or PERT diagramming method. They are:

■ PDM does not have dummy activities since the arrows only represent dependencies.
■ PDM can accommodate any kind of task relationship, including:
  □ Finish to start
  □ Finish to finish
  □ Start to start
  □ Start to finish
  □ Lead and lag
■ PDM is the most widely used network-diagramming method today and all project management software supports it; some, but not all, project management software also supports PERT diagramming.

All network-diagramming methods share a few major disadvantages: they are not understood by everyone, sometimes they are difficult to update depending upon the number and frequency of changes and complexity of the project, and they are not good communication tools. However, they are excellent planning, risk assessment, tracking, and management tools.

Since the PERT method is seldom used any longer (principally because it can only accommodate finish-to-start relationships), only the technique of analyzing a PDM network is shown in this chapter. The analysis for both types is exactly the same, but PDM has become the most commonly used of the network-diagramming techniques and is supported by all project management software packages. The following section describes network analysis in detail using a sample project.

USING PRECEDENCE DIAGRAMMING FOR PROJECT SCHEDULE DEVELOPMENT

Since PDM is the generally preferred and used network tool, only its development and analysis are shown in this chapter. However, the PERT technique will be discussed in Chapter 6 on risk management in information technology projects as a risk mitigation tool. More detailed discussions of PERT and other networking techniques can be found in most basic project management texts.

The first step in developing the project schedule is to estimate the duration of each individual task. Duration estimation should include any contingencies to plan against potential resource shortages. That is, the best-case scenario should not be assumed for the duration, and neither should the worst-case scenario. The duration is usually taken to be the average of similar tasks from the organization's historical database. However, those tasks at risk, relative to potentially unavailable resource numbers or skills, should be planned with a contingency factor. One of the major benefits of the PDM method is that it can accommodate and track this kind of planning, whereas PERT cannot.

Task leaders typically estimate duration and labor requirements, but some organizations prefer the functional managers to make those estimates since it is they who allocate resources and better understand project priorities. Once all task durations are estimated, the next step is to determine task interdependencies.

Determining task interdependencies is a team effort because each task leader will better understand what he or she needs as output from other tasks before his or her own effort can be finished. Task interdependencies drive the schedule because some tasks simply cannot begin until other tasks are completed. For example, the task of system design must be completed before system construction begins. On the other hand, some tasks have no dependencies and can be accomplished in parallel with other tasks. The testing of a completed subsystem, for example, can be accomplished while another subsystem is in development. Careful examination of task interdependencies can shorten the schedule if two or more tasks are done in parallel rather than sequentially, but doing so may add substantial risk to the project, which is the trade-off against potential schedule improvement. If, for instance, a technology survey was planned before designing a critical subsystem, but it was later decided to begin both at the same time and use the survey results to validate the choice of the available technology, there would be an improvement in the schedule. However, if the survey later reveals that the choice of system components is obsolete, then not only is the schedule not improved but the approach likely will have created a schedule slip.

The precedence table lists the tasks of a project or a phase, the tasks that must be accomplished before another task can begin, and the estimated duration of each. The precedence diagram is developed from the precedence table, a sample of which is shown in Figure 4.3. Figure 4.4 shows the PDM representation of the information in this precedence table.

Task alphabetical identifiers are used purely for convenience so that the entire task description does not have to be written on the node. The task leader, based on the experience of previous similar task efforts, usually determines the

Task Alphabetical Identifier	WBS Tasks	Precedence	Task Duration (Weeks)
a	Develop System Architecture	—	4
b	Design Software Modules	a	8
c	Write Code	b	12
d	Design Hardware Subsystems	a	6
e	Build Hardware Subsystems	d	4
f	Write Test Plans	a	2
g	Test Software	c, f	2
h	Test Hardware	e, f	1
i	Integrate Software and Hardware	g, h	3
j	Test System	i	2
k	Install System	j	1

FIGURE 4.3.   Sample Precedence Table

duration of each of the tasks. It is worth repeating that the task duration estimate must take resource availability into account. Otherwise the network analysis to determine the project schedule will be meaningless.

The first step in analyzing any network is to determine the early schedule, which is the earliest each task can begin and end. The early schedule is determined by beginning at node a and working from left to right through each path. This procedure is commonly known as the *forward path analysis*. A path follows the arrows from the beginning to the end of the project. For example, tasks a, b, c, g, i, j, and k are a path. The early start (ES) and early finish (EF) for each task are recorded in the upper left and right corners, as shown in Figure 4.5. Starting at node a, the earliest the task can begin is at time 0. The earliest it can finish is week 4, because the estimated duration of the task is 4 weeks. The earliest that tasks b, f, and d can begin is after task a ends, or after the fourth week. Hence the ES for these three tasks is week 4. Note that these times denote accumulated durations, not calendar time. That is, task b begins after a total of 4 weeks has been expended in the schedule. The ES for each task is the EF of the preceding task except when two or more tasks feed into a task, such as at tasks g, h, and i. When two or more tasks feed into a succeeding task, then on the forward pass that task's ES time is the *larger* of the preceding EF time possibilities. Hence, the ES for task g is 24 weeks because the EF of task c is *larger* than the EF of

Forward Path analysis

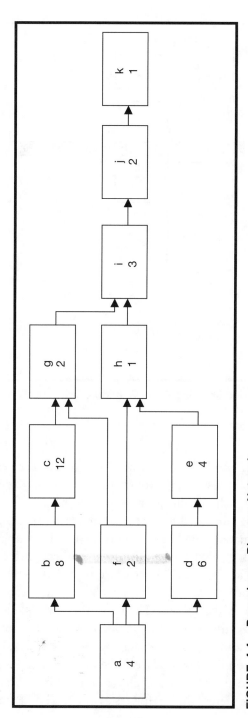

FIGURE 4.4.   Precedence Diagram Network

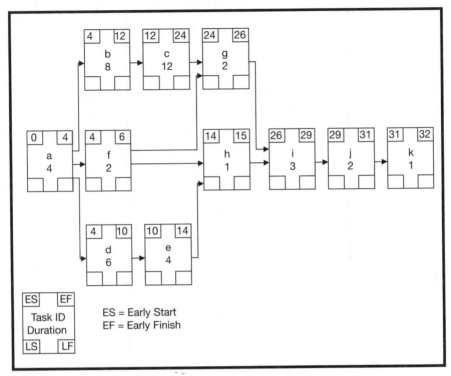

FIGURE 4.5.   Network Showing Early Schedule

task f. Finally, the EF of task k, 32 weeks, determines the schedule for the project. That is, 32 weeks is the earliest that the project can be accomplished—and the shortest time through the network—given the available resources. Figure 4.5 shows the completed forward pass for the network.

Determining the late schedule, or the latest a task can begin and end and still meet the estimated schedule of 32 weeks in the example, is done by working backwards—called the *backward pass*—through the network. The late start (LS) and late finish (LF) times are recorded in the lower left and right corners of each node. To calculate LS and LF, begin at node k by recording 32 weeks in the LF box. The LF of the last node is *always* the EF for that task because the point of the analysis is to determine how late the tasks can be started and ended *without* changing the estimated project schedule. The task duration is subtracted from the LF to obtain the LS for the task. Therefore, the LS for task k is 31. The LF number for each task is the LS of the succeeding task. Thus, the LF for task j is 31. The LS and LF for each task are calculated in the same manner backwards through the network, except where two or more arrows back into a node. In those instances, such as at nodes f and a, then the LF is the *smaller* of the two LS possibilities. The completed network with the early and late schedules is shown in Figure 4.6. The heavy arrows indicate the critical path, or the longest path through the network.

Slack, sometimes referred to as float, is calculated by subtracting the EF from the LF of a task. For example, the slack in task h is LF − EF = 26 − 15 = 11 weeks. Note that tasks a, b, c, g, i, j, and k have no slack. Having no slack on a path is also a defining characteristic of a critical path, and the tasks on it are called *critical tasks.* Critical in the context of network analysis means that if any one of those tasks slips, then the project schedule is affected. Hence, it is critical that these tasks be accomplished on time or ahead of schedule, but not later than planned.

Critical Path - no float

TECHNIQUES FOR COMPRESSING THE SCHEDULE AND LEVELING RESOURCES

Two important uses of the network diagram have not yet been discussed: compressing the schedule and leveling resources.

Methods for Compressing the Schedule

There are two techniques commonly used to compress a schedule. The first is called *crashing* the network and the second is called *fast-tracking.* We will look at fast tracking first because it is relatively easier to accomplish.

Fast-Tracking

This technique involves reexamining all tasks to determine if any that were earlier determined to require sequencing can be done in parallel. In other words, we often decide that a task cannot be started until a particular predecessor is finished, but upon closer examination, perhaps that is not true. For example, suppose a project requires some sophisticated technology, and the first thought was to do a technology survey to ensure that the latest technology available is planned for the project. Now that there is a need to shorten the schedule, a look at the need for a technology survey reveals that

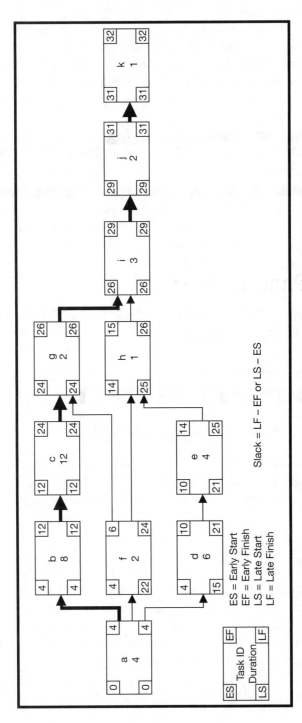

FIGURE 4.6. Completed Network Showing Early and Late Schedules and the Critical Path

such a survey was completed just a month ago. In addition, the project product designers usually keep current with technology changes. Thus the decision is made to do the survey but at the same time start the design and then use the survey to validate the design. Doing both tasks in parallel will shorten the schedule by a week, maybe more.

This scenario is played out every time a project is begun, and it is a good practice to review all task relationships in this way periodically to determine whether the risk of running some of the tasks in parallel is worth taking. *Risk* is the operative word here because fast-tracking adds risk to a project. In the scenario above, if the technology has not changed since the last survey or if the designers truly are up to date on the changes, then the new plan of running the two tasks in parallel will significantly help the schedule. On the other hand, if there were a major change in the technology that the designers did not catch, then the completed survey might indicate a total redesign of the system is required, with a significant impact to the schedule and the budget.

Crashing the Schedule *- reducing duration of tasks*

This technique involves looking at each task on the critical path and reducing the duration of one or more of them. It is good practice to reduce the duration of only one task at a time, but sometimes, in order to get the amount of schedule relief needed, more duration refining than one task can tolerate may be needed.

There are several key points to remember about crashing schedules:

- Pick the tasks on the critical path, because reducing durations in tasks that already have slack in them will not help the overall schedule.
- Reduce the duration by one unit of measure at a time. If the schedule is measured in days, reduce the task by a day; if in weeks, reduce it by a week; and so on.
- Realize that reducing duration usually means adding resources, which adds cost to the project. How much the duration is reduced has a direct impact on the cost of the task, and there has to be a balance between the two.

Figure 4.7 shows an example of crashing a schedule. Remember that one should only work with the critical path tasks when crashing a schedule.

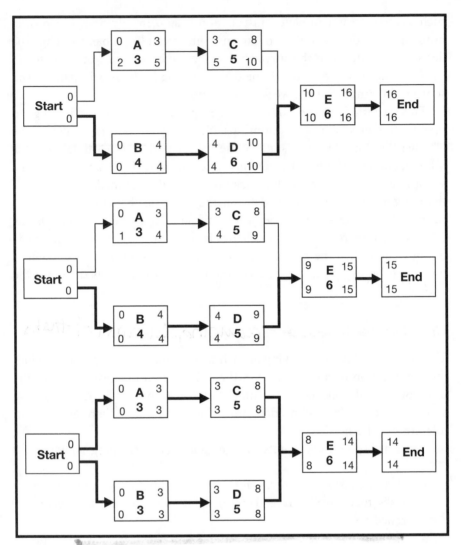

FIGURE 4.7. Crashing a Schedule

Crashing and fast-tracking are the two methods used to shorten a schedule. Generally, neither method is better than the other, and combining the two techniques where possible is usually the better alternative. However, it is important to remember that fast-tracking adds risk and crashing adds costs.

Leveling Resources

One of the major benefits of network analysis is its use as a resource-leveling instrument, and yet it is seldom used for this purpose.

In almost every project, there is always some point during the life of the project when the number of resources needed is greater than the resources available. It simply is not possible to do the work that requires 12 people with only 9 people and keep the project on schedule. What to do? Well, perhaps nothing, but sometimes resource leveling will alleviate the problem, if not eliminate it completely.

Leveling resources, simply stated, involves using the float or slack within a project to reduce the number of resources needed at a particular time period. This does not always work because there may not be enough float to move the tasks enough to achieve the desired results, but it certainly is worth the effort. The process of resource leveling is discussed here, and Figures 4.8 and 4.9 graphically depict these steps.

There is a pattern in resource leveling. The steps are:

- Develop the logic, that is, draw the network for the project or part of the project that needs leveling.
- Determine the early schedule. Determine the earliest possible time each task can begin and end.
- Draw a modified Gantt chart showing when each task begins at its earliest time and, of course, when it ends. Be sure to include float periods and show them as tasks on this modified Gantt chart.
- Develop the resource loading. For each of the tasks in the modified Gantt chart, develop a resource-loading chart that shows exactly how many resources are needed for every period.
- Develop the resource-loading histogram or bar chart to get a clear picture of how many resources are needed and when they are needed. Usually, a resource problem occurs during part but not all of a time period. A resource-loading histogram is an excellent tool for focusing on the critical time period.
- Now determine the late schedule. Determine the latest time each task can begin and finish.
- Draw a modified Gantt chart showing when each task begins and ends at the latest possible time.
- Develop the resource loading as if the late schedule were used.

At this point, there are some options. If using either the earliest schedule or the latest schedule reduces the resource-loading requirements to a level that is supportable, then all you have to do is follow that schedule. However, the most likely scenario is that neither the early nor the late schedule takes care of the problem; it is more likely that some schedule in between the two is what is needed. In other words, use the available float to average the early and late schedules.

Leveling the resources and still maintaining the same overall schedule and not increasing the number of resources requires that float be judiciously placed. That means some tasks are started later, so that the total number of resources required during a particular period of time is reduced.

Leveling is like a puzzle, where float is a piece placed at those times in the schedule that require the highest concentration of resources, during a particular time frame, not on a given task, so that the project still ends at the planned finish date but operates within the given resource requirement. Figure 4.8 is an example of a project network analysis. Notice that task F has some float in the network. Figure 4.9 is an example of how to lay out a project using a modified Gantt chart. The upper half of the example shows the project based on its early schedule. If the available resources are, say, 12 people, then the project will suffer because there is a need for 17 people to successfully complete the project. However, the lower part of the figure

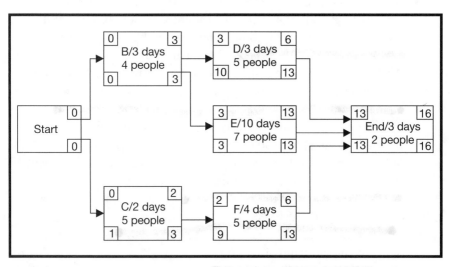

FIGURE 4.8. Sample Precedence Diagram with Duration and Resource Requirements

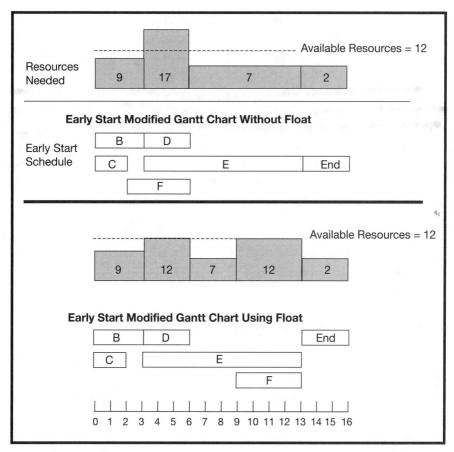

FIGURE 4.9.   Resource Leveling Using Early Start Schedule and Float

shows how to use the float available in task F to level the resource needs so that the needs fit within the framework of people available to work on the project.

This example clearly shows how using the float available can reduce the total resources. But what happens if the resources cannot be leveled without a change in the due date? What can be done then?

Finishing the Scheduling Effort

Leveling resources takes place at different times in a project. It actually first happens during the planning phase, because it will be clear during the first drafting effort of the plan whether sufficient resources exist for the project or for specific times during the project. Therefore, this exercise is not something that just happens because all of a sudden there are not enough resources to do the job; it should be a routine part of optimizing the project plan.

If there is no way the resource load can be optimized to a level that is supportable by the organization, then it is time to review the WBS and to determine whether the project was analyzed and documented correctly and/ or if there is a need to renegotiate the project scope. If the scope cannot fully be renegotiated, perhaps a new, more realistic due date can be renegotiated. Once the final WBS is agreed upon, then there are two more useful project management tools that need to be developed: the Gantt chart and the milestone chart.

Once the PDM network analysis is complete, resource leveling is accomplished, and the final WBS is agreed upon, then Gantt and milestone charts are developed.

GANTT AND MILESTONE CHARTS

Perhaps the most recognized and most used tool in project management is the Gantt chart, and closely behind that is the milestone chart. These two tools are recognized and used by every member of an organization.

Gantt Charts

The PDM provides a network that shows the earliest and latest start and end times for each task and for the entire project. With that information in hand, Gantt charts can be prepared, to graphically show task, phase, and project schedules.

The Gantt chart was developed in about 1917 by Henry Gantt, a pioneer in scientific management. It is a bar chart that shows planned and actual progress for a number of tasks displayed against a horizontal time scale. This type of information display is still one of the most effective and useful tools of project management. In addition to its use as a tracking tool for actual against planned progress, it is a very effective communication tool because it can portray a lot of data quickly to interested parties. Figure 4.10 shows a sample of a Gantt chart that was constructed with Microsoft Project; all project software packages produce similar schedules. In this example, the critical path is shown by a black bar.

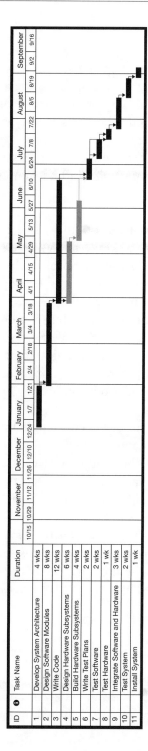

FIGURE 4.10. Sample Gantt Chart

adjust scope
adjust time

ID	⊕	Task Name	Duration	10/15	10/29	11/12	11/26	12/10	12/24	1/7	1/21	2/4	2/18	3/4	3/18	4/1	4/15	4/29	5/13	5/27	6/10	6/24	7/8	7/22	8/5	8/19	9/2	9/16
1		Develop System Architecture	4 wks																									
2		Design Software Modules	8 wks																									
3		Write Code	12 wks																									
4		Design Hardware Subsystems	6 wks																									
5		Build Hardware Subsystems	4 wks																									
6		Write Test Plans	2 wks																									
7		Test Software	2 wks																									
8		Test Hardware	1 wk																									
9		Integrate Software and Hardware	3 wks																									
10		Test System	2 wks																									
11		Install System	1 wk																									

Milestone Charts

Milestone charts are also clear and understandable to almost everyone. Some organizations even try to manage projects using milestone charts as the major management tool. This approach is not recommended because it is not possible to track between milestones to the level of detail needed to actually know what is happening in a project.

Milestone charts can be developed using software packages such as Microsoft Project. In developing milestones, however, it is important to remember the following:

- Milestones have zero duration; they are a point in time.
- Milestones are those events that can be described in the past tense. For example, "getting the project charter signed" is not a milestone; it is a task. "Project charter signed" is a milestone because it is a point in time.
- Milestones are significant events but consume no time.
- Milestones are events that consume no resources.
- Milestone charts are good communication tools because it is easy to relay the sense of progress to senior management by showing that milestones were met on time.

Although many project managers create milestone charts separate from the Gantt chart, it is quicker and more efficient to include milestones on the Gantt chart itself. Then, if the requirement exists, the milestones can be reported in the weekly or monthly status reports. Figure 4.11 shows the previous Gantt chart with milestone points added, usually shown as a diamond shape.

The WBS and network development are the two tools that ultimately lead to every other project management tool. In this section, we discussed not only networks and their importance and uses but also how Gantt charts and milestone charts are derived as a result of the network analysis.

SUMMARY

Scheduling is key to determining the budget, and it is a natural follow-on to development of the WBS. Scheduling may be an iterative process because the customer might need the project delivered by a predetermined deadline.

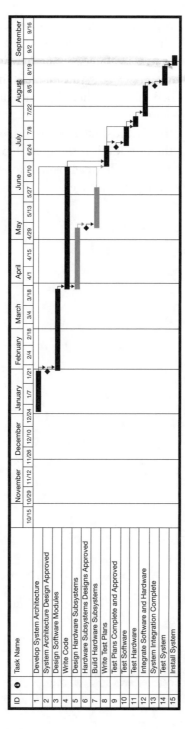

FIGURE 4.11.   Sample Gantt Chart with Milestones Added

To accomplish that, the project manager and his or her team may have to crash or fast-track the schedule in order to shorten the time needed to make good on the deliverables. Network analysis is the best technique for determining schedule delivery or milestone requirements. Once the project team and the customer are satisfied that the schedule is attainable and achievable, the final WBS can be agreed upon.

Remember that the WBS is the first step in project planning, and a network analysis, done at the task level, is the next step. From the network analysis, the Gantt charts, or schedules, can be developed. The next step in the project process is to develop the budget.

5

COST CATEGORIES

It is crucial for project managers to understand cost and cost categories. Most companies depend upon external contracts for their livelihood. Not all project managers become involved in the costing or bidding process—a major oversight in those companies where this happens, but it happens at many. This is particularly true of defense contractors, which do seem to have figured out the right way to gear up for and pursue contracts. This chapter discusses different cost categories and what costs have to be included in a bid and presents some tips for how to structure more competitive price bids.

Accurate costing is key to a company's success; if a company regularly underestimates the costs of its projects, then it obviously will soon find itself out of business. As inane as that statement may seem, there are hundreds of examples of how such a thing can happen. Here are two.

A company in the Washington, D.C. area was steadily losing money in spite of the fact that it was regularly being awarding contracts. Senior management couldn't understand why. This company, as most defense contractors do, hired retired military personnel because the Department of Defense acquisition process is very difficult to understand unless one has worked in it. In this case, the retired military personnel, now project managers for the contractor, were interfacing with active-duty people with whom they had had a long and friendly relationship. That fact by itself is not bad; on the contrary, it can be a marketing plus and is one of the reasons why retired military personnel are hired. The problem was that the contractor project managers, in an effort to accommodate or please their Department of Defense customers, were agreeing to scope changes without insisting on a formal contract change. Consequently, about 30% of the company's contracts were overrunning their budgets—a classic example of scope creep.

In the second case, a private-sector services contractor won a five-year contract to provide engineering and facility maintenance services for a large private firm in North Carolina. A review of the bid price, unfortunately not made until after the contract was awarded, revealed that the company's cost spreadsheet did not automatically sum all the cost columns. Because the total spreadsheet did not fit on the computer screen, the person doing the pricing overlooked two columns of cost figures from each of the five-year contract periods. This oversight cost the company $50,000 per year or a quarter of a million dollars over the life of the contract.

The point of these examples is that there are many ways a budget can be compromised or underestimated completely. The project manager may not be careful in managing the project or, at the other extreme, the estimating process may be flawed. This chapter addresses the most common mistakes and inadequacies in the project-costing process.

MISTAKES AND INADEQUACIES OF PROJECT-COSTING PROCESSES

Some of the most common mistakes or inadequacies in estimating the costs and bidding price of a project are listed in Figure 5.1. These problems are not unique to a particular industry, but generally occur more often in small to mid-size companies. Large corporations grow and become successful in part because they constantly improve their estimating and costing processes. Smaller corporations, however, having less capital, tend to be reluctant to spend the money to train staff in or dedicate staff to the estimating or proposal process, thus making this key function a secondary responsibility. That is, either a senior manager estimates the project costs, usually relying on his or her experience with similar projects, or the technical staff writing the bid proposal also estimates the costs and senior management "refines" them. Either way, estimating accuracy suffers. These inadequacies are discussed in more detail in the following sections.

Problem	Consequences
■ Lack of historical project cost information	■ Each bid starts from scratch ■ There is no baseline for comparing previous failures or successes
■ Technical staff writes proposals as an additional duty	■ Technical staffs are not usually trained to assess or estimate costs
■ Outdated estimating database	■ Cost estimates are inaccurate
■ Reliance on intelligent guesses to estimate costs	■ Almost all estimates are too low; guesses compound the problem
■ Arbitrary cost changes by senior management	■ Even the most accurate cost estimates are negated ■ An unreasonable budget is created (usually too low), and profiles are minimized
■ Underused accounting systems	■ Reporting, database retrieval, and calculating systems are underutilized
■ Management secrecy in sharing labor and indirect rates	■ The staff's ability to assess alternative bidding strategies is reduced

FIGURE 5.1.   Inadequacies of Estimating, Costing, and Bidding Jobs

Lack of Historical Project Cost Information

One of the biggest mistakes any company can make is to neglect the lessons learned from each project. Collecting the lessons learned—what went right or wrong and how the actual work matched the project plan—is where metrics (such as the cost of lines of code to program a software function or the cost of labor measured against experience and skill levels) are recorded, refined, and applied against the next estimating requirement.

It is truly remarkable that so many project and other senior managers do not understand the importance of gathering these data. In the long term, the estimating process suffers, causing a negative, or even a minus, impact to the profit line. Some of the excuses given for not ending a project with lessons learned analyses are:

- There are too few staff members to collect and analyze these data.
- There is no staff adequately trained to accomplish these analyses.
- As soon as a project is finished, project team members are needed to begin a new project; there is no time for a lessons learned analysis.
- Every project is unique, and costing depends on the particular customer or who the competition is.

All of these statements are true, but none are valid. The irony is that lessons learned analysis is relatively easy, and the data already exist from status reports, audits, and budget- and schedule-tracking documentation. All that is lacking is the dedication of two to three hours of the project team's time to go over the data and brainstorm how the project plan could have been improved, why mistakes or errors were made and how they could have been corrected, and, most importantly, how the estimating process could be refined.

Some of the key metrics needed to improve the cost-estimating process are:

- The winner's bid price
- Your bid price
- The winner's track record with the buyer
- Your track record with the buyer
- Ratio of bids won to bids submitted to the customer
- Actual contract or project costs versus the estimated costs
- Efficacy of the risk planning
- Efficiency of the estimating process
- Time allowed to prepare the cost proposal
- Skill and experience of the cost estimate team

Without a dedicated and diligent lessons learned effort and metrics collection, in order to maintain a reasonable business base a company must resort to a shotgun approach to bidding—that is, bidding on as many contracts as possible to win enough projects or contracts to make a profit.

Technical Staff Writes Proposals as an Additional Duty

In small to mid-size companies in particular, and in larger companies occasionally, writing proposals falls to the technical staff as opposed to a dedicated proposal-writing group. What this means to the staff members is that they often have the additional duty of writing a proposal while continuing with their daily duties of running existing projects, administrative functions, and other tasks. Consequently, the proposal and accompanying estimates do not receive concentrated effort from the staff.

The major advantage of having the technical staff write proposals is that these people have the expertise to accurately identify and interpret the customer's requirements and write the management plan. Clearly, that team could make a more accurate estimate, given enough time. But the major disadvantage is that the technical staff has to perform two full-time functions within the same time period, often resulting in overlooked items or tasks.

Outdated Estimating Database

Databases greatly facilitate the costing process, particularly for those companies that provide maintenance services or other services which require materials that are used in the majority of their contracts. A good example of this is facility engineering and maintenance companies. They typically have cost databases with every conceivable spare or replacement item needed to maintain a building. But an outdated estimating database can be worse than having no database at all. Current item costs must be maintained in the database, and new or specially made items also have to be added to the database as they are identified in the requirements.

The company that was responsible for maintaining the Reagan Library did not keep its database up to date and did not realize that the lightbulbs for the library are hand-blown in Belgium—at a cost of $75 per bulb. The company lost a lot of money because it assumed typical household-type lightbulb costs.

Reliance on Intelligent Guesses to Estimate Costs

All project managers and many project team members have been faced with requests to provide a ballpark figure for a task or for a project. There is nothing inherently wrong with such estimates, generally called rough-order-of-magnitude estimates, provided they are made by someone who actually has enough experience and expertise to make an informed assessment of the cost and provided it is clearly understood that this type of estimate is the least accurate method of cost estimating.

Arbitrary Cost Changes by Senior Management

A common problem in those companies that rely on competitive bids for their livelihood is senior management making arbitrary cost reductions to a bid. This action usually occurs after the project team and/or cost estimators estimate the bid price as accurately as possible, but senior management intuitively feels the price is too high to win the contract. Many times, senior management may be right; senior managers usually have a lot of experience and no doubt will have bid on similar projects. However, rather than arbitrarily reducing the bid by some percentage across the board, which often means the wrong item or task cost is reduced, it is far better to continually "scrub" the cost proposal until the overall costs are legitimately reduced to an acceptable level. Using this approach will tell senior managers whether the costs can be reduced to their level and avoid laboring under an unreasonably low budget if the contract is won. Otherwise, one never knows, until after the project is started, whether the arbitrary cost reduction was reasonable or even needed.

Underused Accounting Systems

Accounting and other management information systems are improving at a rapid pace, and most companies, particularly those dedicated to training and supporting project management as a way of doing business, are using their systems to provide lessons learned and estimating support. Still, all too many controllers and accounting department heads maintain that their primary function is to track corporate costs, taxes, and profit-and-loss information, which is certainly true. However, given the functionality of today's accounting systems, not fully utilizing them to store, retrieve, and analyze important project data reduces a company's ability to improve the costing process.

Another common complaint from project managers relative to their companies' accounting policies is that many accounting departments require all expenditure and revenue reports to go through the accounting process first rather than through the project. Of course, this practice delays a project manager's ability to maintain current budget status by, in some cases, as much as a month; a project could be over budget and no one would know it until a month later. The simple answer to this problem is to set up a system in which both the accounting department and the project team have access to budget information at the same time or at least the information is provided to the project manager on a timelier basis.

Management Secrecy in Sharing Labor and Indirect Rates

There has long been strong paranoia within the corporate hierarchy about sharing or talking out loud about company rates for labor and indirect costs, that is, overhead and general and administrative (G&A). There is good reason for this paranoia—the competition. Overhead and G&A rates are often the difference between two competitive bid prices, and it is natural to want to protect such proprietary information. The problem for the project manager and the cost estimator, if they are not among the select few who have access to these rates, is that it is not possible to compare the estimated project costs to the target bid price without having these rates. Although I do not advocate that you broadcast your rates, we will see later in this chapter that a competitor can easily compute your cost and price factors, which essentially provides the competitor with your overhead and G&A rates; likewise, you can compute a competitor's rates, and I'll show you how to do it. In short, there is a lot of secrecy for nothing.

COST ESTIMATING DEFINED

There are probably as many definitions of cost estimating as there are cost estimators, but the simplest and most direct definition comes from the Society of Cost Estimating and Analysis, which defines cost estimating as "the art of approximating the probable cost of something based on information available at the time." Many view cost estimation as an art; others view it as a process. My personal bias is that cost estimating is a process, principally because "art" implies a nebulous, guessing kind of a system whereas "process" suggests that, with the right approach to estimating, the result has more of a scientific basis for the final cost estimate. Whether you view cost estimating as an art or a process, though, its purpose is to predict future costs based on today's knowledge, which, by the way, can be different by tomorrow.

The methods and techniques described in this book are built on the basis of a process, and there will be constant reminders to reestimate your costs as a project progresses because, as with any other plan, the cost plan changes as the project changes or as more exact information is known.

Difference Between Cost and Price

Too often, the terms "cost" and "price" are used interchangeably, indicating a basic lack of understanding of what each word means. Costs include labor rates, materials, equipment, travel, consultants, overhead, and G&A expenses. Simply stated, price equals costs plus profit or fee, which brings up another question. What is the difference between profit and fee?

If one interviews those people in an organization who write proposals or makes contract bids and asks them to describe the difference between a fee and a profit, the majority of those decision makers will proclaim that they are one and the same. It is remarkable how few people actually recognize there is a difference between the two, but almost no one can explain the difference (accountants and other professional financial practitioners can of course, but most people who write contracts and proposals are not financial professionals). In most cases, understanding the difference makes little or no difference. Most companies either add a fee or calculate a profit and add it to the bid, but they usually use one or the other so there is no confusion. In some cases, though, not understanding the difference could mean large losses for a company and severe job repercussions for someone who does not understand the difference.

One company sent a contract administrator to negotiate a contract with the specific instruction not to negotiate lower than a particular *profit* rate. This person assumed fee and profit were the same and negotiated a contract with a *fee* rate equal to the desired profit rate. The result was that the company lost several thousand dollars and the contract administrator nearly lost her job. What is the difference? It is in the definition of the terms.

Fee is based on cost; profit is based on price. Thus, the difference is in the application of the rates. Say, for example, all the labor, materials, over-

Fee - based on cost
Profit - based on price

head, and G&A for a project total $1,000,000. If the company typically adds a fee to the cost to determine the price, then it simply means that some fee percentage is applied. For convenience, assume the company wants a 10% fee. The price, then, is:

Total cost	$1,000,000
Fee (0.10 × $1,000,000)	$100,000
Price	$1,100,000

But now let's say the company wants to realize a 10% profit on the contract. The price is decidedly different, and here is why. Profit, by definition, is the difference between the final price and the original cost. Mathematically, it is described in this way:

$$Cost = Price - Profit\ rate \times Price$$

In other words, there is some percentage rate of the price that is the amount of profit, and subtracting it yields the original cost.

Rewriting the equation to determine what the price must be to realize a particular profit rate, it becomes:

$$Price(1 - Profit\ rate) = Cost$$

or

Profit

$$Price = Cost/(1 - Profit\ rate)$$

Using the earlier example, in order to get a profit of 10%, the price would have to be:

$$Price = \$1,000,000/(1 - 0.10)$$
$$= \$1,000,000/0.90$$
$$= \$1,111,111$$

Thus, in this case, the difference between a 10% fee and a 10% profit is $11,111.

Profit calculations are always higher because they are based on the price, not the cost. Now it is easy to see why the contract administrator erroneously negotiated a lower contract price because she thought fee and profit were the same thing. It pays to know the difference between the two and how to explain the difference in order to clarify senior management directives. Let's look at another example.

One company decided to bid on a very large, multiyear contract. Because of the complexity of the project and the competition involved in the bid, it was decided that a consultant, known for his creative cost and pricing strategies, would be hired to structure the project cost proposal. Although company officials were involved throughout the costing effort, they did not realize that when the consultant was told to include a 15% profit, he did not question whether they really meant fee. The result was a bid price that was significantly higher than the competitive range.

The estimated project cost was approximately $25,000,000. If bid at a 15% fee, the cost would be:

$$\text{Bid price} = \$25,000,000(1 + 0.15)$$
$$= \$25,000,000(1.15)$$
$$= \$28,750,000$$

But when bid at a 15% profit, the cost would be:

$$\text{Bid price} = \$25,000,000/(1 - 0.15)$$
$$= \$25,000,000/0.85$$
$$= \$29,412,000$$

The resulting bid was nearly $662,000 greater than intended because senior company officials did not know the difference between fee and profit. Not surprisingly, the company lost the contract.

TYPES OF COSTS AND COST CATEGORIES

Types of costs and how to aggregate them into the various cost categories established by the government or by private-sector cost-accounting standards can be confusing to even the most experienced project manager—and hopeless for the new or less experienced project manager. Defining the primary terms associated with cost types and the various cost categories can help immensely.

Direct costs
Indirect costs
Fixed costs
Variable costs
Semivariable costs
Other direct costs
Life cycle costs
Operating and maintenance costs

FIGURE 5.2.   The Most Commonly Used Cost Categories

There are several cost categories that are used in cost estimating and in collection of cost data. Grouping costs into common categories satisfies different needs for cost data. For example, depending on the decision at hand, management may want to see cost estimates categorized by phase of the life cycle, frequency of occurrence (nonrecurring versus recurring), or cost allocation (for example, direct versus indirect). Figure 5.2 lists the most commonly used cost categories. Detailed explanations of each are provided in the following sections.

Direct Costs — specific contract or project

Direct costs are all those costs that can be associated with a particular cost center or, in simpler teams, a specific contract or project. These costs include labor, materials, equipment, services, and fees that are directly chargeable to accomplishing the objectives of a project. A key characteristic of direct costs is that they must be traceable to show clearly that they are, in fact, directly associated with a particular project and no other.

Indirect Costs

Indirect costs are those costs not directly identified with a single final cost objective. Rather, they are identified with two or more final cost objectives. Specifically, the indirect cost category is further subdivided into:

- **Overhead**—That part of business associated with the well-being and comfort of employees. For example, office space and furniture, heating, air conditioning, and lighting all contribute to the comfort of the employees. The costs of these amenities and the associated taxes and insurance are overhead costs.

■ **G&A**—The costs of doing business associated with the health and well-being of the company. For example, senior management, marketing and new business development personnel, accounting staff, company lawyers, and a proposal development staff are all G&A labor because the work they do is for the benefit of the entire company, not a single contract.

■ **Benefits**—The cost of doing business associated with providing benefits such as a company car, health and medical programs, and tuition reimbursement. Many companies combine the benefits category with the general overhead category.

Fixed Costs

Fixed costs remain constant on a total basis, regardless of production volume, and remain the same even if production temporarily stops. Fixed costs include rent, depreciation, managerial salaries, and insurance. For example, general plant maintenance costs tend to be fixed from month to month, regardless of how many units are produced in a given month. Machine maintenance costs will also be fixed up to a point, but clearly will be affected more by quantity of output being processed on a machine. This cost might be considered a semifixed cost.

Variable Costs

Variable costs are a level and type of cost that change according to the amount and nature of work performed and include such costs as raw material expenses, wages, freight charges, and sales commissions. For example, labor hours to build a particular piece of hardware are expended only if materials are being processed by the machining function and thus would vary according to how much the machine, in this case, is used.

Semivariable Costs

Semivariable costs fall between fixed and variable costs in that they are neither entirely fixed nor entirely variable; they may vary directly, but not proportionally, with changes in production volume.

Let's say, for example, that costs associated with financial transactions for a student population, which seemed to be fixed for a certain range of activity (say, 11,000 to 13,000 students), suddenly become variable because student numbers doubled. Such costs are semivariable costs, reflecting the fact that they may vary with significant changes in the level of activity.

Other Direct Costs

One category of direct costs that confuses most people is other direct costs. The reason for the confusion is that the costs that make up this category commonly are classified as indirect costs, but for a special reason it makes good sense to charge these items directly to a project contract. Some very common examples include plant or building protection, transportation, packaging and shipping, certain supplies, telephone and computer expenses, consultant fees, and clerical expenses. All of these functions and costs typically fall into the category of indirect costs. However, if any indirect cost item can be clearly identified and measured as being dedicated to a project contract, then it usually can be classified as a direct charge, and the government or other accounting standards organizations will accept it as such. Again, the key is being consistent in the application of such costs to other projects within the company and supplying supporting data to justify the categorization of what are usually indirect charges as direct charges.

The principal difficulty with the other direct costs category is not in determining whether a cost could legitimately be classified as an other direct cost but rather in ensuring that the cost is not duplicated in the indirect cost pool. In other words, every company will have a pool of typical costs that make up the indirect cost pool. When an item is classified as an other direct cost, the cost should be analyzed to make certain that it is not already included in the indirect cost pool. The indirect cost pool has to be reduced by the amount of any other direct costs.

Life Cycle Costs

Life cycle cost elements reflect the entire project life cycle. Typically, there is an overlap of life cycle phases, but the costs can be identified with a certain phase based upon the effort they reflect. The acquisition portion of the life cycle is complete when a system is placed into operation. Therefore, the total project acquisition costs refer to those costs incurred in the project development and implementation phases. Acquisition costs may include the purchase of an initial set of repair parts (usually a one- to three-year supply depending on the size, complexity, and length of service expected from the project product), even though these costs really should be considered a part of the operation and maintenance phase. Once the ultimate user takes ownership of the system or services, the actual operating and maintenance phase begins, and any costs incurred consist of the operating and maintenance costs.

Operating and Maintenance Costs

Operating and maintenance cost is exactly what it sounds like—the operation and maintenance of a delivered system. An example of operating and maintenance costs would be the manpower costs to operate an air traffic control tower; the cost occurs year after year as air traffic controllers use the terminal. Likewise, the equipment and tower facilities are also maintained as they are used and suffer from wear.

DEVELOPING A COST-ESTIMATING PROCESS

The best cost-estimating system is based on databases derived from historical data. These databases contain labor, materials, facilities, and equipment costs that are current and accurate. The cost-estimating process description should emphasize the accuracy and timeliness of the information. If a company can point to several contracts that were accomplished on time and on budget using its costing techniques, the customer will be more confident that the company can deliver. A flowchart depicting the costing process is the best way to describe how the system works. Figure 5.3 presents a sample costing process that could be used to develop a winning cost estimate.

Understanding the competitive environment is key to successful bidding. As a company understands more about its environment, a powerful proposal process can be developed. The key to winning contracts is a powerful, and accurate, costing process.

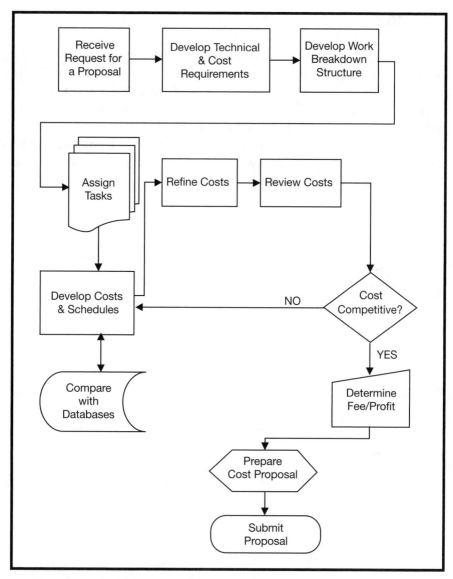

FIGURE 5.3.   Cost-Estimating Process

SUMMARY

Competing for contracts is one of the most challenging forms of business endeavor any company will ever encounter. Many companies are unable to survive in this environment simply because of the knowledge, experience, patience, perseverance, and creativity needed by their employees to produce consistently winning technical and cost proposals.

The most critical function in any company's effort to compete and gain a major market share is its ability to accurately assess the competition and to consistently offer solid cost proposals.

6

ESTIMATING AND BUDGET DETERMINATION

Perhaps the single greatest challenge in project management is allocating resources across projects within the organization and, consequently, estimating schedules and costs with any accuracy. There are tools and techniques available to help the project manager accomplish these tasks, and this chapter discusses them in some detail.

The beginning to any successful resource allocation and estimating effort, though, is always the requirements analysis and the resulting scope and work breakdown structure (WBS) development. Assuming the project manager has a well-developed WBS and the schedules are as accurate as possible, given available information, the next step is to assess skills needed and number of personnel. It should be obvious at this stage of the process that schedules and costs are not mutually exclusive but rather have to be developed somewhat together in order to arrive at the final budget estimates.

RESOURCE PLANNING FUNDAMENTALS

When the resource-planning effort begins, there are some very fundamental questions that need to be answered. These questions all come out of the requirements analysis. The key questions include:

- **What needs to be done?** This question goes right to the heart of the project requirements. Simply put, what are the deliverables? Only when the deliverables have been identified can the project manager determine what personnel, equipment, and materials are needed.

- **Who and what are needed?** If the deliverables are firmly identified, an assessment of the skill sets, experience levels, and equipment or materials is possible. At this point, the project team can determine whether the organization has the required expertise in-house, and if not, what outside help is needed.

- **Who can do the work?** Identifying the skills and experience requirements is only half the battle; marrying the skills and experience with those available to work on the project is the challenge. Organizations optimize their resources so that none are idle, at least not for extended periods, so finding people with sufficient skills and experience can be a project in itself.

- **What can do the work?** Many projects are labor intensive; some require capital equipment, special machinery, and other materials. This question addresses those issues and is important to the overall costing and schedule effort.

- **Who and what are available?** Just because particular skills, experience, and equipment are needed does not mean that they are readily available; they may be allocated to other projects or they may not be available at all in the organization. The trick is to balance the need with what is available in a way that does not jeopardize any project.

- **What level of excellence and competence is essential?** This question really addresses three issues. First, what are the skill sets and experience levels needed to do the job at all? Second, what is the minimum level of skill sets and experience needed to meet the quality standards of the project? Third, what level of skill and experience is needed to accomplish the work in the time required by the customer?

- **How are the resources used?** Once the resources are identified, the decision has to be made about their utilization. If, for example, the people assigned to the project do not have the level of skill and experience desired, they might have to be subsidized with senior-level resources or longer shifts may be required.

■ **How will the resources affect schedules and costs?** Regardless of the resource mix, it is a fact that the schedules and costs will be directly affected. If senior people are used, even for short periods, the costs will go up; if less skilled and experienced people are used, the schedule will be longer, which also increases cost.

It is easy to see that resource planning is the key to optimizing the schedule and costs, but there are other considerations in resource management too.

RESOURCE MANAGEMENT CONSIDERATIONS

Once resources are identified and assigned, there are some immediate actions the project manager should take. One is to develop a resource/responsibility matrix and the other is to use the resources to help develop estimates.

Resource/Responsibility Matrix

The resource/responsibility matrix (Figure 6.1) is a management tool to help the project manager know "who is doing what." That is, it is a matrix with key personnel matched against the WBS tasks. Usually, only the key task people are listed in the matrix, but it can be expanded as needed. It really is a management tool that can be as detailed as necessary for monitoring and controlling a project.

At a minimum, the WBS task and the task lead will be identified in the resource/responsibility matrix, but it is always a good idea to include key support, review, and approval personnel. With enough information in the matrix, the project manager can easily track where the work is and when it is expected to move to the next level.

Resources as Estimating Sources

Resources are a vital source of information about how long a task will take and how much it will cost. There is a push by the Project Management Institute and other organizations to rely more on estimating tools or expert judgment than on individual team members. The rationale is that people within an organization tend to err on the side of pleasing management or,

RESPONSIBILITY MATRIX					
Project Title: _____			**Project Manager:** _____		
WBS Entry	**Task Lead**	**Primary Team Member Responsible**	**Secondary Team Member Responsible**	**Inspection Authority**	**Sign-Off Authority**

FIGURE 6.1.   Sample Responsibility Matrix Form

worse, are afraid they might not be able to hit their estimates and therefore inflate them. The truth is probably somewhere in between. People responsible for a task generally will have a better understanding of how long it will take and how much it will cost. The project manager should take their input, but also should validate it using other methods such as estimating tools, expert advice if it is available, and, above all, historical or lessons learned data. Estimating is not a trivial pursuit; it should not be done using only one method or tool. The more methods and techniques used, the more accurate the estimate.

DURATION

Settling on a consistent definition of time is an age-old battle. The problem in considering duration is that almost everyone has a different view of time. Generally, when estimating how long it will take to accomplish a task, project teams estimate optimistically because they tend not to consider risk and tend to assume there will be no interruptions or phone calls, all the resources will be available, and so on. Also, there is a tendency to ignore or forget that everyone needs personal time; no matter how good or skilled the worker, each person is productive for only a particular amount of time per day. Therefore, when estimating durations, it is important that the project team and the stakeholders all agree on working calendars, hours per shift, and holidays and also allow for such things as sick leave, vacation, and productivity in the estimate. Otherwise, the estimate will start off too optimistic, which has been shown to be the case in almost every project regardless of the industry.

What are some of the duration considerations to be mindful of in estimating schedules and the attendant costs?

Duration Considerations   Need consistent definitions

It is amazing how many duration estimates are wrong because of a lack of consistent definitions in an organization or even across an industry. This is partially because everyone has their own definition of the various terms relating to duration, and no one takes the time to ensure consistency. This problem is easily eliminated; it just takes agreement on definition of terms and enforcement of use of the definitions across the organization.

The following are key important, and troublesome, terms:

- **Effort hours**—The number of hours required to complete a task or project. Effort hours are usually expressed in days, weeks, months, or years, depending on the context. When an estimate of effort to accomplish, say, a task is made, the effort can be expressed in terms of resource hours or days. For instance, if a task is expected to take 16 hours of effort, then it would take 2 resource days.

- **Working hours**—The number of hours available to do work in a day or week. The working hours are defined by the organization or team and established before the project begins. Of course, working hours can be changed depending on the need to make up schedule slippage. The standard workday is 8 hours and the standard workweek is 40 hours, but working hours are defined as needed by the project. Shortening or lengthening working hours has no effect on the effort hours; it just shortens or lengthens the elapsed time it takes to complete the work.

- **Elapsed time**—The actual passing of time. It includes weekends, holidays, breaks, vacations, and so on. It is simply calendar time, everything included.

- **Productivity**—The rate at which one does work. Everyone has a rate at which they can accomplish a task. Generally, more skilled and more experienced people will exhibit a higher productivity rate, but skill and experience do not guarantee greater productivity. It is not hard, though, to measure productivity across an organization and to use an average number. The productivity rate commonly used in many industries is 75% productivity, but this number can vary by industry and by organization based on actual historical records.

- **Availability**—Simply when and whether a resource is available for work. It really doesn't matter if someone is 100% productive if he or she is not available to do the work—the work cannot be done.

- **Contiguous duration**—Uninterrupted work time. Contiguous duration is important because once started some tasks can be irrevocably damaged if the work is interrupted. If a project involves building a concrete foundation, for example, pouring half the foundation one day and finishing it a few days later would create air pockets, weak spots, and other structural problems.

■ **Interruptible duration**—Work time that may be interrupted. That is, when building a house, there is no real harm in putting up one wall one day and another wall the next. In fact, even building half a wall a day will not jeopardize the integrity of the structure.

All the definitions and concepts listed here are important, but two that are seldom considered in estimating a schedule are productivity and availability. These two concepts need to be understood and applied in every estimate.

Productivity and Availability

Assigning productivity to individual workers carries with it the potential for litigation. To be safe, it is better to assign an average productivity figure across the entire organization when making time and cost estimates. However, for the sake of demonstration of the formulas, it is informative to see how productivity and availability affect cost and time when a comparison of three workers with different productivity levels and different availability times is made.

The formula for determining cost is:

$$\text{Cost} = (\text{Effort/Productivity}) \times \text{Unit cost}$$

where effort = project or task resource hours required, productivity = percentage (expressed in decimals) one is productive in a day, and unit cost = labor cost in dollars per hour for the resource.

As an example, suppose a project manager needs to know the labor cost for one individual whose hourly rate (i.e., unit cost) is $30 and productivity is 85%; the effort is projected to take 40 hours, and this person is only available 75% of the time. The cost of using this person for 40 hours would be:

$$\begin{aligned}
\text{Cost} &= (\text{Effort/Productivity}) \times \text{Unit cost} \\
&= (40/0.85) \times \$30 \\
&= \$1,411.76
\end{aligned}$$

To determine how long it will take the person to do the task, use the formula for calculating the time required:

$$\text{Time} = (\text{Effort/Productivity})/\text{Availability}$$
$$= (40/0.85)/0.75$$
$$= 62.75 \text{ hours}$$

Even though the effort required is only 40 hours, it will take about 64% longer to complete the task using this person who is 85% productive (which is actually very good) and can only work on the task 75% of the time because of other project commitments.

It is easy to see, then, that by following the usual instinct to provide cost and time estimates based only on an individual's base hourly rate and assuming 100% productivity and availability, the estimate would be 40 hours to do the work and the cost would be $1,200 ($30 an hour × 40 hours). Herein lies one or the biggest reasons for estimating errors.

It was stated at the beginning of this section that assigning individual productivity rates potentially leads to litigation. This is so because assigning productivity rates can lead to, or be perceived as, discrimination.

To further demonstrate the power of, and need for, using productivity and availability rates, consider the following example, which compares the cost and time of another individual for the example above. Worker 2 has an hourly rate of $35, a productivity rate of 90%, and is available 85% of the time. The cost for worker 2 is:

$$\text{Cost} = (40/0.90) \times \$35$$
$$= \$1,555.56$$

The task will take worker 2:

$$\text{Time} = (40/0.90)/0.85$$
$$= 52.29 \text{ hours}$$

Which of the two workers would be the better choice for the task? That decision depends upon whether cost is the driving factor, in which case worker 1 would be better (cheaper), or whether schedule is the most important factor. If schedule is a driving factor, worker 2 can do the task about 10.5 hours faster for only about $144 more.

The industry standard for figuring productivity is 75% productive based on a 40-hour week. This productivity rate is determined by recording the actual amount of time an average individual spends on his or her assigned tasks and taking into account the amount of time required for meetings, administrative work, breaks, and other normal office interruptions. Availability is determined by assessing how much time a person would have for a particular task given the amount of time already committed to other work activities.

Once the task/project effort is determined, resources are identified and assigned, and productivity and availability rates are known, the job of estimating the costs and schedule can begin in earnest.

[handwritten annotation: Standard productivity = 75% of 40 hour work week.]

ESTIMATING

Estimating costs and schedules is not an easy task. Traditionally, all project costs and schedules will be optimistic; that is, in the end, a project is usually over budget and behind schedule. This overestimating is more prevalent in some industries than in others, but it occurs everywhere. This section discusses different approaches to estimating, some tools and techniques for developing estimates, and some suggestions for how to improve the estimating results.

Two definitions need attention: cost estimating and cost budgeting. These two terms are often wrongly used interchangeably, probably because people tend to think of "costs" as one category and "price" as another without considering that there are levels of costs and price. Therefore, this section will, among other things, provide an explanation of these confusing elements of the estimating, proposing, and budgeting process.

- **Cost estimating**—Determination of the resource costs needed to accomplish project activities. Resource costs include all labor, equipment, materials, and any other resources needed to do the job.
- **Cost budgeting**—Allocation of the approved budget to individual tasks or activities.

The principal reason for making this distinction is that the process of actually allocating budget amounts to specific tasks provides a basis for tracking how well the budget is doing against the plan. Cost estimating can be done in several different ways and is not always done based on the individual task level. Hence, in a case where the estimate is developed at a higher level, it is only when the budget is allocated to each individual activity that a clear picture of how good the estimate is begins to emerge. Therefore, the cost estimate alone is not sufficient to baseline the project and to track and manage the work as it progresses.

Types of Estimates

Estimates can be grouped into one of three categories within the WBS: the top levels of the WBS, middle or summary levels, and all levels of the WBS. Within each of these categories, there are several techniques commonly used in the estimating and organizational environment. The different types of estimates and their levels of accuracy are shown in Figure 6.2.

There are two important points to be made about this graphic. First, the three levels have vastly different degrees of accuracy associated with them. As the estimating methods or techniques drill down from the top of the WBS to the lowest level, the accuracy improves. Second, take note of the precision and range of accuracy associated with each of these levels. These

Estimating Technique	Description	Accuracy
Rough order of magnitude	■ Top level ■ Conceptual, ballpark ■ Low accuracy	−25% to +75%
Top down	■ Mid level ■ Budgetary proposal, contractual ■ Better accuracy	−15% to +25%
Budget or engineering	■ Work package level ■ Definitive, based on real work effort and resources ■ Best accuracy	−5% to +10%

FIGURE 6.2.   Levels of Estimating Accuracy

ranges were developed from studies published by the Project Management Institute, and they represent the accuracy of projects from all industries across many organizations. There are three things about the different ranges that are noteworthy:

- The variance decreases as the estimate type becomes more detailed.
- They clearly indicate the tendency to err on the optimistic side.
- Whenever possible, it is better to give an estimate range when providing cost data.

Estimating Recommendations

The following are important tips, or recommendations, for preparing estimates:

- Use the most accurate estimating method available.
- Use two or more methods if possible to validate the estimated costs.
- Involve the entire team and any other experienced personnel available to develop the estimates.
- Base the estimates on lessons learned, which, if properly documented, will provide data to refine estimating techniques.
- Record *all* assumptions.
- Communicate the level of precision of the estimates to the stakeholders.
- Do not pad the estimates; use contingency costs if risk is a potential, but clearly identify the contingency strategies as separate costs.

Estimating Tools and Techniques

There are many estimating tools and techniques available to the project manager and his or her team, but most of them fall within the ones mentioned in this section.

If a project is labor intensive (which means it basically consists of only the labor effort), such as a service contract, then the costs are generally not too difficult to determine. It is a matter of determining the length of the service effort and multiplying that number by the number of resources and their individual labor rates to arrive at the total. Unhappily for most of us, estimating the cost of most projects is not so easy, and it usually takes the combination of several different tools and techniques to arrive at an accurate estimate. Basically, there are two approaches to estimating a project's cost: the top-down and the bottom-up estimating techniques.

The top-down approach is usually less accurate, but not always. It is a function of how experienced the estimator(s) is and what methods are used to arrive at the top-down figures. Generally, however, the top-down estimate is less detailed, as it relies principally on analogy for the results, and is often used for project selection or a rough indication of project cost, what a potential bid price might be, and for determining general strategies and planning approaches.

The bottom-up approach is more detailed because it goes to the very lowest levels of the WBS and costs the individual work packages. As each work package is assigned a cost and duration, the costs are *rolled up*, or summed, to the next highest level of the WBS until all activities are assigned a cost. The final rolled-up number is then the cost of the entire project.

Within each of these approaches, there are several tools and techniques available, as follows.

Analogy

Analogy involves comparing one project or subelement to another similar project or subelement. The analogous estimating technique is referred to in the *PMBOK® Guide* as *being also called top-down*. This is a very misleading statement because it implies that these two terms are synonymous. The fact is, analogy can be used at any level of cost or schedule estimating.

As an example, suppose a company is contracted to build a house similar to one it built last year. To get a rough estimate of the cost of the new house, the project manager can compare the size, location, and general amenities of the two and come up with a comparable cost, provided the two houses are similar enough and in comparable geographic locations.

Parametric Modeling

Parametric modeling looks at one measure in terms of another. Parametrics are used every day. When buying wallpaper, for example, the basic considerations, after determining the total square yardage of the area to paper, are how many feet or yards there are per roll and how much the rolls cost in terms of dollars per roll. Both of these measures— feet per roll and dollars per roll—are parametrics. They are parametrics because one measurement is expressed in terms of another. Parametric estimating is also called a cost-estimating relationship because of this relationship of one measurement in terms of another.

As an example, suppose your organization builds concrete driveways. Over the past three years, sufficient data have been collected to develop a parametric to determine the cost estimate for a new driveway: 1 yard of concrete costs $50 per yard. The estimate for a contract to pour a new driveway that requires 200 yards of concrete is $10,000 (200 yards × $50).

Vendor Bids

Vendor bids compare the bid price of one vendor against another. Notice that the word *price* is used here. The difference between cost and price is that additional money in terms of overhead and profit is added to *cost* to obtain *price*. This subject was discussed in Chapter 5 in detail. If evaluating vendor bids as a part of a larger contract, then the vendor's total price is considered a part of the cost of winning the contract.

As an example, suppose an information technology project requires 50 computers and three vendors bid on the contract to supply them. If the requirements and specifications are accurate (i.e., computer capability, time and place of delivery, service, reliability, and so on), then the discriminator in evaluating the bids is cost. If the bid prices are $100,000, $98,000, and $95,000, then the winner would be the $95,000 bid, and this price becomes part of the larger bid.

It is clear, then, how important it is to understand cost categories and types of costs. It is not enough to just determine what the different costs in a project are; they have to be allocated to the correct *pot* of money because of accounting and financial restrictions and standards.

Project Reserves

One other very important budget consideration is project reserves. Reserves are used to ensure a project stays on track, and if something should happen (i.e., a risk event), then money or schedule contingencies are in place to get it back on track.

Reserves historically come in two forms: contingency reserves and management reserves. The Project Management Institute once differentiated between contingency reserve and management reserve. It has, however, discontinued that practice for two reasons. First, it was confusing because unless an organization constantly deals with these terms, it is difficult to distinguish between the two. Second, and probably the most important reason, many organizations do not distinguish between the two—they just lump all reserves into one category. It is important, however, to distinguish between the two because some customers are very picky about the use of reserves, in particular when dealing with the federal sector.

Contingency Reserve   *Contingency - cover ID'd risks*

A contingency reserve is usually money, but it can be schedule, to be used if an identified risk event occurs. These risk events are identified during the planning phase, and contingency strategies are developed. If a risk event occurs, funds are available to implement the strategies and to get the project back on track. Contingency reserve is planned into the project budget and is usually, but not always, under the control of the project manager.

Management Reserve   *for unexpected risks*

Management reserve is a reserve that is set aside for unknown risks. This reserve usually is determined by applying some percentage factor to the overall project contract and is controlled by senior management. It is not a part of the project budget, and its use usually requires a briefing to senior management on the need and approval to tap into the reserve.

Reserve is not a fudge factor or budget padding. Padding the budget is not acceptable practice according to the Project Management Institute, most organizations, and certainly the customer.

PROGRAM EVALUATION AND REVIEW TECHNIQUE

Finally, there is the question of what to do when the cost or duration of a task is unknown. In virtually every project, there comes a time when the best anyone can do is only guess about the cost or the schedule. A tool that minimizes this subjectivity in determining the cost or duration would be a very nice thing to have at hand, and there is such a tool. It comes from the program evaluation and review technique (PERT) method developed in the 1950s for just such events.

PERT was the first diagramming method developed to mitigate risk in estimating schedules, and the same method can be used to mitigate the risk in estimating costs. Everyone who has formally studied or read about project management and the tools of project management knows about PERT, but it is important to review the concept in terms of how it can be used to estimate deterministic schedules and costs.

The PERT formula is:

$$\text{Estimated time (or costs)} = [\text{Optimistic} + (4 \times \text{most likely}) + \text{pessimistic}]/6$$

Simply stated, this formula says that if one can provide three time (or cost) estimates—the most optimistic, the most pessimistic, and the most likely, then a time (or cost) that mitigates, to some degree, the risk of a guess can be determined.

This formula is actually a beta curve, but it approximates a bell curve distribution, which is more familiar to most people. Two engineers compared hundreds of Department of Defense contracts and project plans and their results to derive the formula, which would have provided a more accurate estimate than what was used in the original project planning. The PERT formula is the result of their research.

The formula is easy to use. There must be three estimates, which are best obtained from the person in charge of doing a task. Say that person thinks that optimistically the task can be done in 10 weeks and at the outside 18 weeks. However, the most likely time will be 16 weeks. (Keep in mind that instead of duration, this could be cost as well.) What is a reasonable duration for planning? The PERT formula provides an estimate of the task duration:

$$\text{Estimated time} = [10 + (4 \times 16) + 18]/6$$
$$= 15.3 \text{ weeks}$$

There are some things that need to be recognized about this result. First, it is a weighted average. The reason why the most likely estimate is multiplied by 4 is that the developers of the formula realized that this number needed to be more heavily weighted and, if viewed from the perspective of a bell curve, weighting the most likely number moved it closer to the mean. The second thing that needs to be recognized—and planned for—is that the estimated time, 15.3 weeks, falls near the mean of the beta curve, which is what the PERT formula describes. Therefore, there is only a 50% chance that time will be achieved. Hence, there needs to be some method for improving the chance of decreasing the risk in the estimate. This brings up the concept of the standard deviation.

Standard Deviation in PERT Estimates

Fortunately, there is a way to improve PERT estimates, and it has to do with the statistical determination of how far removed from the mean the actual duration is. This is easily seen from Figure 6.3.

The formula for the standard deviation away from the mean is given by:

$$SD = (P - O)/6$$

where SD = standard deviation, P = pessimistic estimate, and O = optimistic estimate.

Using the pessimistic and optimistic estimates from the estimated duration calculation, the standard deviation is determined to be:

$$SD = (18 - 10)/6$$
$$= 1.33$$

Studying Figure 6.3 closely, it is clear that by adding one standard deviation to the mean, the chance of hitting the schedule improves to approximately 85%; 50% of all data points fall to the left of the mean and 34% fall between the mean and the +1 standard deviation point—hence 84 or approximately 85%. Approximately 85% is used because one of the Project Management Institute's favorite questions on the PMP® certification exam is: Below what point on the bell curve do approximately 85% of all data points fall? Or, alternatively, above what point on the bell curve do approximately 15% of all data points fall? The answer to either question is +1 standard deviation.

If two standard deviations are added to the PERT-estimated duration, then the probability of hitting the schedule is improved to about 98%. Thus, to improve the probability to 85%, the schedule should be, for the example

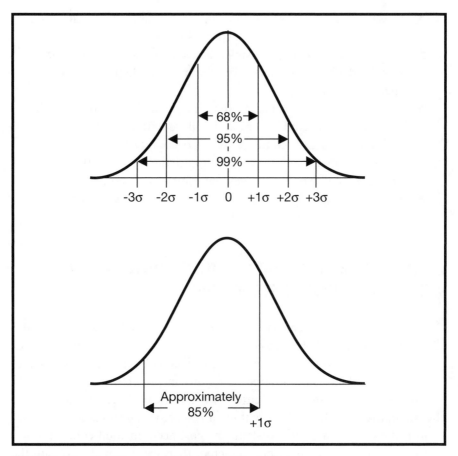

FIGURE 6.3. Bell Curve and Standard Deviation

above, 15.3 + 1.33 = 16.63 weeks; to increase the probability to 98%, it would be 15.3 + 2 × 1.33 = 18 (rounded).

FINALIZING THE ESTIMATES

Once an estimate is completed, the following checklist items ensure that nothing was overlooked:

- Make sure to check everything.
- Redefine what the requirements are, and make sure that all requirements are included in the WBS.

- Closely study the assumptions and constraints, and make sure they make sense and have been considered.
- Validate, to the extent possible, data sources, and ensure that all stakeholders agree on the estimating methodology and precision characteristics.
- Identify the cost drivers, and determine whether changes can be made that will reduce them and still be within the target costs.
- Estimate reasonable contingency reserves, and determine whether the project manager has authority to use them to keep the project on track or if senior management approval is required.
- Make sure that whatever the cost, it meets the customer's expectations and budget constraints.

COLLECTING COST DATA WITH THE INTEGRATED WORK BREAKDOWN STRUCTURE

One of the best ways to collect cost data is to use a WBS that incorporates all the components of the project. Figure 6.4 is a sample of such a WBS, which is easily constructed in Microsoft Excel. Once a template is developed, it is easily modified to accommodate follow-on projects.

To use the integrated WBS, enter all the work packages in the leftmost column of the worksheet, along with their respective control accounts. Enter each of the control account totals in the cost account total column. Once all the control accounts have been entered, they are summed to obtain the total project cost estimate.

SUMMARY

Perhaps the biggest challenge facing a project manager and his or her team is planning resources in such a way that no project in the organization is adversely affected and that the resources are adequate to develop project budgets and schedules. Resource planning is crucial because the consequences of poor resource allocation are projects over budget or behind schedule or both.

There are essentially two ways to estimate a project cost: top down or bottom up. Top down is less accurate because it depends on experience, but

Project: _____
Project Manager: _____

Estimator: _____
Date of Estimate: _____

Page _____ of _____

WBS No.	WBS Description	01 Engineering Labor	02 Manufacturing Labor	03 Systems Engineering	04 Facilities	05 Purchased Parts	06 Test Equipment	07 Tooling	08 Configuration Management	09 Software Development	10 Hardware Development	11 Integration and Assembly	12 Quality Assurance	13 Test	14 Subcontracts	15 Packaging	16 Integrated Logistics Support	17 Project Staff & Administrative Support	18 Graphics Support	19 Reproduction	20 Shipping and Handling	21 Consultants	Cost Account Totals	Total Project Cost

FIGURE 6.4.   Integrated Work Breakdown Structure, Work Package, and Cost Accounts

it also depends on analogy, which is only as good as how closely two projects compare. The bottom-up method, which starts at the task level and rolls up to the final project cost, is by far the most common estimating method, but still is only as accurate as the data provided by the task leaders. There is a tendency to pad the estimates because of unknown risks or the fear that senior management might reduce individual task budgets. Numerous cost-estimating software packages are available, but they are only as good as the data input into them.

Both cost and schedule estimates depend upon an understanding and consistent use of several terms:

- Effort hours
- Working hours
- Elapsed time
- Productivity
- Availability
- Contiguous duration
- Interruptible duration

Even the best project managers and estimators sometimes reach a point when they really do not know how to make a reasonable estimate. The technique most often used to mitigate the risks in these situations is the PERT technique, which depends upon three estimates to arrive at a weighted average. The technique also provides for a simple calculation for standard deviation to improve, or mitigate the risk of, the duration estimate.

Finally, an integrated WBS is used to collect project costs. It is an efficient means of combining the WBS with each of the costs associated with a project and provides the project manager with both a communication and management tool.

7

PLANNING
THE PROJECT

The project plan is produced during the planning phase. Although planning starts much earlier—even during the concept phase and requirements definition, the plan cannot be finalized until reasonable estimates of schedules and costs are made.

The project plan is the formal document that guides execution of a project. Planning occurs throughout a project; that is, the planning process is dynamic and ongoing, and many planning processes will be repeated during the design and execution phases as changes are made in the project. This chapter will focus on that time at the beginning of a typical project when the bulk of the planning functions are accomplished.

The project plan is not a file created and stored in a scheduling software package. The project plan is a dynamic document that coordinates all the various processes and project-planning documents used to manage and control a project. The project manager must understand how to develop a plan that addresses the core processes related to scope, schedule, and cost, as well as the facilitating processes related to risk, procurement, human resources, communication, and quality. The project plan also generates many subsidiary plans, which also are discussed in this chapter. Finally, risk management is discussed in this chapter as well because it is during the planning phase that risks are identified and documented.

ıvıany problems can occur in a project if insufficient time is spent planning; the purpose of planning is to prevent those problems from occurring. Causes of poor planning may include estimates that are poorly done; exception handling that is grossly misunderstood; requirements that are incomplete, changing, or not understood; technical complexity that is misunderstood; old code content that is not known; new requirements that are added or sneaked into the plan; dictated constraints; and inadequate time to do a proper job.

Typical planning problems include:

- Unanticipated risks
- Dependencies not accounted for
- Insufficient detail to manage the project
- Lack of clear intermediate checkpoints
- Lack of detailed content for each checkpoint
- Inadequate time allowed for design
- Inadequate time allowed for verification and rework
- Configuration management started too late to be effective
- Test development started too late to be effective
- Design that is not user friendly
- Difficult transition into the user's environment

The effects of such planning problems may include missed checkpoints and milestones, loss of credibility, inability to defend against unreasonable requests, inability to evaluate the effect of changes in requirements, shortcuts taken in design, shortcuts taken in validation (such as reviews, inspection, and unit testing), more design errors than anticipated, more rework than expected, and staff, skills, and expertise not available when needed.

SCOPE PLANNING

The *PMBOK® Guide* (page 375) offers the following key definitions related to planning the scope of a project:

- **Scope**—The sum of the products and services to be provided as a project.

- **Scope planning**—The process of progressively elaborating the work of the project, which includes developing a written scope statement that includes the project justification, the major deliverables, and the project objectives.
- **Scope statement**—A documented basis for making future project decisions and for confirming or developing common understanding of project scope among the stakeholders. As the project progresses, the scope statement may need to be revised or refined to reflect approved changes to the scope of the project.

The project manager gets the scope, in general terms, from the project concept phase. Is it well defined? Does it make sense? If not, the project manager should seek clarification about how it was developed, particularly if he or she was not involved in the development or did not participate in discussions with the customer, whether internal or external.

The primary output of scope planning is the scope statement, which should include:

- **Project justification**—The business reason for the project
- **Project deliverables**—Products and services the project will produce and their characteristics
- **Project objectives**—Quantifiable criteria that must be met in order for the project to be considered successful

The scope statement is the basis for the work breakdown structure (WBS). A detailed discussion of WBS development is provided in Chapter 3.

SCHEDULE PLANNING

Schedule planning helps project managers manage the time side of the triple constraint. The project team might be faced with a specific deadline and forced to work backwards from the overall project duration to figure out how to schedule each work package. This would be analogous to a top-down approach to building a WBS. A bottom-up method of building the schedule, which starts with the durations of individual work packages and builds them into an overall project schedule, is preferable because it is more accurate.

The objective of schedule planning is not simply to show when activities are expected to be performed, but also to show how project components relate to each other and how a change in one may or may not affect others. This information can then lead to smarter decisions during the implementation phase.

Three common scheduling techniques are used: network diagrams, Gantt charts, and milestone charts. Some are more effective than others depending upon the complexity and size of a project.

Regardless of the scheduling technique used, the durations of activities in the schedule must be estimated. This is best done from the bottom up, especially for network schedules, which are defined by the activities, their logical dependencies, and their durations.

When estimating durations, it is important to understand precisely the type of durations being discussed. Normally, estimates are converted from hours to days. For example, suppose an information technology development activity is estimated to take 48 hours. The time for the scheduled activity would be 6 workdays if an 8-hour workday is being used. If a Monday through Friday workweek is being used, that workweek can be built into the schedule, and the total calendar days elapsed would be 8 days.

Returning to the 48 hours of work time and the 8-hour workday, consideration should always be given to the resources assigned. For example, could two people perform the activity together in 24 hours and reduce the duration to 3 workdays? This sort of effect is much less likely in information technology than it is in fields such as construction, where additional manpower or equipment can often speed up performance.

Productivity and availability are other important resource concerns. If the developer assigned to the activity is only allowed to work on the project half time, it will take twice as long to complete the activity. Conversely, if one developer is twice as efficient as another, the duration of the activity must be estimated accordingly.

CALCULATING PRODUCTIVITY AND LABOR AVAILABILITY

Assigning individual productivity rates to individual workers risks litigation. To avoid this problem, apply an average productivity figure based on the organization's productivity rate or find an average for the industry. For purposes of demonstrating the following formula, 75% productivity (a good average across most industries) is assumed.

The formula for determining cost is:

$$Cost = (Effort/Productivity) \times Unit\ cost$$

where effort = project or task resource hours required, productivity = percentage (expressed in decimals) a person is productive during a day, and unit cost = labor cost in dollars per hour for the person doing the work.

Suppose we want to know the labor cost for a task estimated to take 1 week or 40 hours to be completed by an individual whose hourly rate is $20 and whose productivity rate is 75%. Further, assume that this individual can only be available 75% of the time because of other project commitments. What is the cost of this individual and how long will it actually take him or her to complete the task?

From the above formula, the cost is:

$$Cost = (Effort/Productivity) \times Unit\ cost$$
$$= (40/0.75) \times \$20 = \$1,142.86$$

To determine how long it will take this person to do the job, the following formula is used:

$$Time = (Effort/Productivity)/Availability$$
$$= (40/0.75)/0.75 = 71.11\ hours$$

Clearly, if we were to follow our basic instinct and provide cost and time estimates based solely on an individual's base hourly rate and assume 100% productivity and availability, then the estimates would be 40 hours to do the work and $800 ($20 × 40 hours). Herein lies one of the major reasons for cost and schedule estimate errors.

After the task or project effort has been determined, resources have been identified and assigned, and productivity and availability rates have been calculated, the job of estimating the costs and schedule can begin in earnest.

GANTT CHART

The Gantt chart is one method of showing project information. It a bar chart that depicts activity durations from left to right as horizontal bars plotted on a calendar grid. Normally it shows the original project plan, but parallel bars depicting actual progress can be plotted next to the planned activity bars for comparison.

The biggest advantage of the Gantt chart is that it is very easy to understand. This is particularly true for people who lack formal project management training, and this has made it the most common scheduling technique.

MILESTONE CHARTS

Milestones are key points in a project that mark some significant accomplishment. For example, they can denote accomplishment of logically related tasks, completion of a certain percentage of work, or expenditure of a certain amount of labor hours of effort or a certain amount of funds. Unlike activities, they consume no time, money, or resources. It is ideal to have milestones that occur every four to six weeks within a project schedule.

Because of their simplicity and their focus on major accomplishments, milestone charts are useful for senior management and provide high-level views of project status. They are similar to Gantt charts because they plot the milestones against a calendar. The only difference is that the milestones represent points in time rather than durations of ongoing work activities.

ESTIMATING

Estimating is the bridge from the WBS to planning schedules, costs, and resources. The *PMBOK® Guide* provides a definition of and describes different types of estimating within several of the knowledge areas, for example activity duration estimating within project time management and cost estimating within project cost management. The basic process of estimating applies to the wide variety of estimates needed in projects, including time estimates for scheduling, cost estimates for budgeting and personnel, and equipment estimates for planning resources.

At times, estimating seems to be as much art as science, yet it is essential to good project planning. The validity of the estimates heavily influences the smoothness of the project and the likelihood of being on target or suffering overruns. Some project team members may suggest that estimating is unimportant or a waste of time because everything will change anyway. The project manager should not let the team go down this road. Carefully developed estimates help keep projects on track by providing performance measures and permit more logical incorporation of changes into the plan.

Why Is Estimating Difficult?

There are many causes of poor estimating. Sometimes poor technical judgments are made because of the instability of requirements or new technology. Work that involves new technology is always difficult to estimate accurately because of the lack of historical references. Estimators also may lack the necessary experience in a particular area. When a project is being done for an external customer, an intentionally low estimate may be provided in an effort to receive the contract award. If the requirements are not totally defined or agreed upon from the start, it will be very difficult to estimate aspects of the project accurately. In some projects, changes are not controlled, and the baseline is not adjusted when approved changes occur. Regardless of the reason, providing inaccurate estimates or not estimating at all is likely to result in major problems in a project.

Good Estimating Practices

Estimates range from ballpark to highly detailed figures. The project manager should determine what kind of estimate can be provided based on the time and resources available. A high degree of accuracy is not always possible or desired. For instance, if a new client in beginning discussions asks general questions to find out whether the cost is in keeping with plans, a general ballpark estimate is in order. To develop specific project budgets, however, more accuracy is required. Whenever an estimate is shared with others, the level of detail and accuracy being provided should be clearly conveyed along with the estimate.

Sources of information for estimates include files from previous projects, employees with special expertise, supervisors, and consultants, among others. Other excellent sources, which have recently become more widely available, are the databases of professional organizations. These organizations keep historical data for their industry or area of interest. With Internet access to the Information Technology Association of America, for example, one can obtain excellent data about information technology projects. That being said, it is still wise not to rely on any one source. Instead, gather information from as many sources as possible.

Many tools and techniques exist to prepare estimates, but regardless of which is used, bottom-up estimating based on the WBS will give the most reliable results. This should be kept in mind throughout the planning process, since poor or unnecessarily vague estimates will inevitably negatively affect the scheduling, budgeting, and resource-planning processes that rely on them. The order in which those three aspects of the project plan are developed may vary depending on the nature and constraints of the project. Ultimately, however, they all must be coordinated so that they are consistent with each other.

COST ESTIMATING

After all the resources and task durations are estimated, costs can be determined. The *PMBOK® Guide* defines cost estimating as "the process of developing an approximation of the cost of the resources needed to complete project activities."

The major sources of input for the cost-estimating process include the following:

- **Resource requirements**—These should have been determined already.
- **Resource rates**—Generally specified by the accounting or finance department.
- **Duration estimates**—In addition to factoring into the cost of resources, these estimates may affect the estimate when the project budget includes an allowance for the cost of financing.
- **Chart of accounts**—Any numbering system used to monitor project costs by category (for example, labor, supplies, materials). It is usually based on the corporate chart of accounts of the primary performing organization.
- **Historical information**—Includes previous project files, commercial estimating databases, and project team knowledge.

Note that the cost of the project management activities, especially if subcontractors are used, can be significant and is frequently overlooked.

These management costs and other administrative costs for project support functions must be recorded as project costs. For example, training for the project team can be a major cost component, especially if out-of-town travel is required.

Types of Cost Estimates

The major types of cost estimates are order-of-magnitude estimates, budgetary estimates, and definitive estimates. They vary primarily based on when they are done, why they are done, and how accurate they are.

The rough-order-of-magnitude estimate is developed very early in a project, usually in the concept stage. It is often done to help make project selection decisions. Its accuracy is typically +75% to −25%, which means that the project's actual costs could be 25% below or 75% above the estimate. Ideally, this sort of estimate is not developed until after requirements have been identified. In reality, it is often developed before that, which can be dangerous and explains why estimates can grow dramatically from the first estimate to the second.

Top-down estimating is usually done when the high-level design is completed, which is still fairly early in the project life cycle. The accuracy of the estimate is between +25% and −10%.

A budgetary or engineering estimate is usually developed after the detailed design has been completed. It should provide the most accurate estimate of project costs, within a range of +10% to −5%.

Building a Cost Estimate

Like building a WBS, building a cost estimate can be done by using a bottom-up or a top-down approach. When using the top-down approach, the cost of large segments of work (for example, development or testing) is estimated. This can be done by using industry rules of thumb or by comparison to the actual cost of previous similar projects. The advantages of this approach are that it can be done quickly and that, theoretically at least, it does not overlook the costs that transcend individual work packages. Its obvious disadvantage is that because it uses a very broad approach and is often used by people who are not very familiar with the work to be done, it is not very precise. It will result in the sort of variances that fall within the range expected from order-of-magnitude estimates, since it is one way of developing them.

In the bottom-up approach, the WBS is the key to cost estimating, just as it is in all other planning processes. Ideally, it should always be used to organize cost estimates and to ensure that the costs of all identified work packages are estimated. The essence of the bottom-up approach is to develop the WBS and then assign cost estimates at low levels and accumulate them to determine the project's total cost. The advantage of this approach is its accuracy, which lies in the range expected for a definitive estimate. Its accuracy stems from having people who know the work provide the estimates and from its focus on much smaller and more precisely defined components of work.

Done properly, the best estimate is certainly a definitive, bottom-up estimate. However, these estimates do take considerable time and effort to develop, and they can present problems if certain mistakes are not avoided. For example, people providing such estimating data as work hours required to perform a given task may feel compelled to include more hours than they really need to do the work. The project manager must not allow this, since it will grossly skew the overall project estimate. The project manager also must not forget to include in the estimate indirect costs that are not associated with particular work packages. Leaving out these project overhead costs will quickly lead to cost overruns.

Cumulative Cost Curve

Cumulative cost curves are graphic representations of the planned expenditures for a project. Time periods are measured along the x-axis, and cumulative costs expended at any particular time are measured along the y-axis. Connecting the cumulative cost points of a project during each time period over the entire duration of the project plots a line graph. Since plotting project costs by time period in a noncumulative fashion usually produces a bell curve, with higher expenditures during the middle of the project and lower expenditures at the beginning and end, the cumulative cost curve usually takes the shape of a somewhat flattened "S." Accordingly, it is often referred to as an S curve. Figure 7.1 is an example of an S curve.

The cumulative cost curve is valuable because it can help the project manager see the total planned budget and communicate it in a shorthand

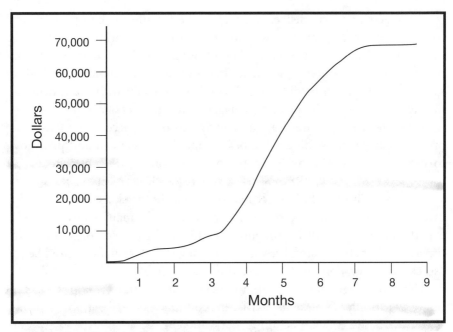

FIGURE 7.1. Sample Cost or S Curve

way. It can serve as an excellent briefing tool because most people can easily read the graph. It can also serve as an excellent way of summarizing progress, since both planned and actual cost curves can be tracked on the same graph for comparison purposes. This also proves useful in connection with the concept of "earned value," which is discussed in Chapter 9.

RESOURCE PLANNING

The project plan needs to account for various kinds of resources, including people, equipment, and facilities. Senior management and the core project team play particularly significant roles in resource planning. In many organizations, senior management must garner resources from other divisions of the company on behalf of a project. If a project requires contracting outside resources, the person responsible for contract management will be an important person to work with. In addition, the core project team, through its own contacts and experience, is often the best route to the optimum resources. Functional managers who are responsible for various departments in the organization will often be key resource providers. Through them, resources like computer equipment, administrators for clerical help, office space, and so on can be obtained. A good relationship with the functional managers can make the project manager's life much easier.

Ultimately, people are the reason why a project succeeds or fails. The project manager must obtain the best people he or she can and plan how to use them most effectively. In the planning phase, the focus is on the specific individuals who are to be recruited for the project team. The resource plan will help the project manager identify the skills needed for the project and when they are needed. For example, in many cases, a testing expert will not be needed throughout the life of the project, only at certain times. One benefit of careful resource planning is that it can help avoid being "stuck" with someone just because they are available.

There are several tools a project manager can use in planning resources: the responsibility assignment matrix, the resource spreadsheet, the resource Gantt chart, the resource-loading chart, and the resource-leveling chart.

Responsibility Assignment Matrix

The *PMBOK® Guide* defines the responsibility assignment matrix as "a structure that relates the project organization breakdown structure to the work breakdown structure to help ensure that each component of the project's scope of work is assigned to a responsible person." The responsibility assignment matrix is a very useful tool from a project management and control standpoint, as well as a good communication tool for the project team and stakeholders. By plotting tasks against staff on a matrix and labeling each person's assignments as primary or secondary, it provides a quick and easy view of who is primarily responsible for each project component and who may provide support.

Resource Spreadsheet

A resource spreadsheet lists the various types of resources being used and allocates the quantity of each resource by time period. Normally, you would want a relatively smooth resource curve that starts with a small number of people, increases, reaches a peak at the height of project activity, and then quickly drops off at the end. It should be similar to a bell curve.

Resource Gantt Chart

A resource Gantt chart is a bar chart that groups activities according to the resources required to perform them. Normally, the Gantt chart is a cascade of activities in chronological order by start date. In this case, the activities are grouped first by their assigned resources and then by chronological order within these groupings. A resource Gantt chart is of good use to functional managers in determining staffing possibilities.

Resource Loading and Leveling

A resource-loading chart is a histogram (vertical bar chart) that shows the planned allocation of people by time period. Time periods are measured along the x-axis, and quantities of resources are measured along the y-axis. The amount of resources to be used according to the project schedule during any given time period is depicted by a vertical bar; the taller the bar, the greater the amount of resources. This type of histogram makes it easy to detect peaks and valleys in the use of resources and apply the scheduling technique known as resource leveling.

The *PMBOK® Guide* defines resource leveling broadly as "any form of schedule network analysis in which scheduling decisions (start and finish dates) are driven by resource constraints (e.g., limited resource availability or difficult-to-manage changes in resource availability levels)." Very often, when resources are assigned at the work package level, the resource-loading chart based on a network schedule shows significant ups and downs in the application of resources. This can be difficult to manage, since having resources join a project, perform as required, and then depart is usually the most desirable and efficient way to use them for all concerned.

Resource leveling addresses this problem. It takes advantage of float time in the project schedule to allow certain activities to be performed later than planned, thereby permitting a smoother buildup of resources. Of course, this may not always work. It is entirely dependent upon how much float is in the project. Whenever float is used to level resources, the risk of critical project delays increases. This is another effect of the triple constraint. In this case, seeking an advantage in resource management creates a disadvantage in time management.

RISK PLANNING

A risk, according to the *PMBOK® Guide,* is "an uncertain event or condition that, if it occurs, has a positive or negative effect on a project's objectives." Risk identification and analysis take place throughout the life of a project. They were factors in project selection (as discussed previously), they become part of project planning, and they are ongoing parts of project execution and control.

In planning a project, do not try to plan for or expect every possible scenario; at the same time, do not ignore the bad things that have a reasonable probability of happening. Procurement delays, loss of a key employee, and equipment failure are typical project risks. Also do not forget good risks! These are opportunities, and the project manager needs to be in a position to capitalize on them if they arise. Examples might include a special equipment discount from a vendor or the availability of the company's best developer because of the early completion of another project. Project managers who prepare for good risks look good when they capitalize on them, and, unlike "bad risks," good ones tend to disappear quickly if they are not seized upon.

Risk Probability and Impact

There are two key questions to ask in risk analysis: How likely is a risk to occur, and what will its impact be if it does occur? For example, suppose the probability of a server failing and having to be replaced is 20% and the result would be $10,000 in additional costs and one week of project delay. Without such a clear understanding of probability and impact, one does not have a basis for dealing with the risk from a planning level.

The various combinations of probability and impact presented by different risks should be used to prioritize them. A risk's level of priority will determine the degree to which responses to the risk are planned for. Obviously, one would plan for a 60% risk with a $10,000 impact differently than a 10% risk with a $5,000 impact. There might be a risk of a power blackout disrupting a project, but is it worth much response planning?

Risk Response Strategies

After evaluating the probability and effect of each risk, the project manager needs to decide how to respond to it. The *PMBOK® Guide* offers the following four basic risk response strategies from which to choose:

- **Avoid**—This means changing the project plan to eliminate the risk or condition in order to protect project objectives. One way of doing this would be to eliminate some aspects of the project scope.
- **Transfer**—This means shifting the consequences of the risk to a third party. Commonly, this is done through insurance or the use of contract terms that assign risks to other parties. For example, a fixed-price contract may place the burden of certain cost over-runs on the contractor.
- **Mitigate**—This means reducing the probability or impact of the risk to an acceptable threshold. For example, you might decide to build in more testing of a new piece of software before you release it.
- **Acceptance**—This means deciding not to change the project plan to deal with the risk, either because it is not deemed to be serious or because it is considered to be a cost of doing business.

To sum up, it is crucial for the project manager to identify and analyze risks and put together a risk management plan as part of project planning. Keep reviewing the risks, their priorities, and the best response strategies available based on the best information throughout the course of the project. Remember that everything can change as a project progresses.

SUBSIDIARY MANAGEMENT PLANS

Subsidiary management plans are often found as part of the overall project plan. They typically consist of the following:

- Communications management plan
- Procurement management plan
- Quality management plan

Communications Planning

Many stakeholders, including the project team, have different needs for information about a project. Many considerations will go into the communications plan. The more visible a project is, the larger the communication task will be, but every project has various target audiences.

The key is to plan how information will flow during the project. Who gets what types of information? Who gets a weekly status report? Will it be sent only to your boss, or will it be sent to the vice president? How will communication tools be used? What will the role of e-mail be? Will an e-mail list be set up, with perhaps a few groups to get news out quickly? Many companies use e-mail for information but not for tasking. What meetings will be held and who should attend them? Will there be weekly staff meetings? How many team members will be involved in them? Will a section on the company's intranet be needed? This is just a sampling of the types of issues that should be addressed by a good information technology project communications plan.

Procurement Planning

Increasingly, project managers are called on to procure goods, services, and labor for their projects. Procurement planning involves determining which project needs can be best met by procuring products or services outside the project organization. This is similar to the so-called "make-or-buy" decision. It also involves consideration of how to procure, what to procure, how much to procure, and when to procure. The major output of procurement planning is a procurement management plan.

Procurement and its legal ramifications can be complex. It is best to work with the professionals within an organization to get this right. However, knowing the basics helps the project manager to make good selections that can be implemented correctly with the assistance of in-house professionals.

There are various situations where outsourcing should be considered. They include when an organization lacks the capability or expertise necessary to perform the work, when it is desirable to share the risk with an outside organization, when it is cheaper to outsource, and when an organization does not want to incur the ongoing expense of hiring full-time staff for a discrete and short-term component of a project. If the decision to buy is made, key factors to consider in source selection include cost, reliability, and timeliness of work. If material or equipment is being purchased, key factors to consider are quality, availability, and when it is needed. If people are being hired, key factors to consider are the right expertise for the job and a good reputation.

Different organizations have different ways of dealing with procurement. Some are very formal and centralized and have a contracting office that plays a key role. Others may be more informal and decentralized and give the project manager greater discretion. It is important to know how an organization views contracts, in terms of centralized or decentralized, and to accommodate the organization's approach. Both approaches have advantages and disadvantages, so a unified organizational approach is crucial to consistent management practices.

Quality Planning

Quality refers to both project deliverables and project management. For example, you might be able to deliver a product by the deadline, but if you do it by forcing your team through 6 weeks of 14-hour days, that may have negative consequences on product quality as employees get fed up over the long term. Because the importance of quality often gets lost in the rush of deadlines and budget cuts, the project manager should emphasize it from the planning processes through project closeout.

In the end, only the customer can really define and evaluate the quality of your product. The customer will evaluate your product whether you like it or not, and that evaluation will determine future business. If you are not planning to influence that evaluation, you will lose!

Certain characteristics of any project tend to affect quality, especially the following:

- **Functionality and features**—Functionality is the degree to which a system performs its intended function. Features are the special characteristics that appeal to users. It is important to clarify which business functions and features the system must perform and which functions and features are optional.

- **System outputs**—These are the screens and reports that the system generates. It is important to clearly define what the screens and reports look like for a system. Users must be able to easily interpret these outputs and get all of the reports they need in a suitable format.
- **Performance**—This addresses how well a product or service performs the customer's intended use. For example, what volumes of data and transactions should the system be capable of handling, how many simultaneous users should the system be designed to handle, and what type of equipment must the system run on?
- **Reliability and maintainability**—Reliability is the ability of a product or service to perform as expected under normal conditions without unacceptable failures. Maintainability addresses the ease of performing maintenance on a product. Most products cannot reach 100% reliability, so stakeholders must define what their expectations are.

Special Subsidiary Management Plans

Subsidiary management plans might include, for example, a security plan, which documents the activities and methods that will be followed to ensure system security. Typically, a security plan will cover issues such as data encryption, passwords, access levels, and so forth.

Other typical plans might include:

- **Logistics plan**—Describes what methods will be used to deliver the product/system to the client/customer (timing, shipping, installation)
- **Transition plan**—Describes how the product/system will be transferred to the customer/client and covers issues such as user training and customer acceptance
- **Configuration management plan**—Covers issues such as documentation control, quality assurance, releases, versions, and test scripts
- **Test strategy plan**—Describes how system functionality will be tested

THE PROJECT PLAN

The culmination of all this planning is the project plan. The project plan provides the road map to the design and construction phases of a project. It wraps up all the planning already done: the WBS, scheduling, costing, resource planning, risk and procurement planning, communications planning, and quality planning. Each project will also have its own special subsidiary management plans, such as the transition plan, configuration management plan, and test strategy plan.

When all the components of the project plan have been documented, they must be put together in a completely coordinated manner. Although the format and content of the project plan will vary somewhat by organization, the value of having it to use as a guide and reference document cannot be overstated. Without a project plan, a project will be a disaster; with one, there is a reasonable chance of success. Figure 7.2 is a generic format for a project plan.

PROJECT MANAGEMENT PLANNING SOFTWARE

Software tools can be very helpful to the project manager, but they do not take the place of human thought and talents. Basic business software such as word-processing, presentation, database, and graphics applications can be used as well by a project manager as they can by any other businessperson.

In addition, there is a whole family of programs specifically designed to help with managing projects. Although they speed up many time-intensive tasks, one should not rely on them without understanding the concepts of scheduling, risk, quality, and other aspects of project management that underlie them. Using software without understanding it is like letting a baby play with a calculator. Numbers are keyed in and calculations are made, but they do not do anyone any good.

SUMMARY

Planning is key to project success. It is estimated that approximately 50% of a project's budget is spent during the planning process.

    I.   Executive Summary
   II.   Project Description
       A.   General Description of the Project
       B.   Project Objectives
       C.   Project Fit with Strategic Goals
   III.   Technical Approach
   IV.   Contractual Requirements
    V.   Resource Requirements
       A.   Equipment
       B.   Materials
       C.   People
   VI.   Schedules
       A.   Master Schedule
       B.   Detailed Phase Schedules
       C.   Milestone Chart
       D.   Deliverable Schedule
       E.   Meetings or Other Customer-Required Schedules
   VII.   Cost Estimates and Budget
  VIII.   Potential Risks
   IX.   Evaluation Criteria
    X.   Appendices
       A.   Systems Engineering Management Plan
       B.   Risk Plan
       C.   Communications Plan
       D.   Logistics or Other Special-Purpose Plans

FIGURE 7.2.   Generic Project Plan Format

The whole purpose of planning is to eliminate or anticipate errors or risk events that could happen to move a project off track. The key to successful project planning is to completely understand the scope, which means understanding customer requirements. From the scope, a WBS is developed so that everyone clearly understands what is required to accomplish the project objectives.

Perhaps the most difficult part of project planning is making reasonably accurate schedule and cost estimates. One way to ensure accuracy is to account for productivity and availability. There are some simple formulas to calculate these numbers, and they help provide reasonable cost and schedule estimates.

One of the major problems in planning is accounting for risk events. A thorough risk analysis is crucial to ensuring successful project completion.

Finally, it is important to realize that a project plan generates several additional plans, such as the communications plan, procurement plan, quality plan, and risk management plan. Usually, these plans are attached as appendices to the project plan.

THE IMPLEMENTATION PHASE

The word implementation is a little misleading because it implies simply putting something into motion, but it is more. It is considered the main phase of a project—the phase during which the actual work is performed. This is the phase in which the project product is started, monitored, and controlled.

Project *implementation* is the process of putting the project plan into action. A project plan is a road map for how a project should progress; project implementation turns the plan into reality.

Monitoring is the process of assessing project performance or how a project is doing against what was planned. Very quickly, it will become apparent to the project manager and team just how well they have planned the project when they start measuring actual against estimated performance.

Controlling is the process of managing the deviations from the plan. During the planning phase, such key things as the project budget and schedule are determined. Controlling the progress of a project means controlling how closely the actual expenditures and work accomplished follow the planned solution.

This chapter and Chapter 9 on earned value management comprise the implementation, monitoring, and control aspects of project management. Generally, earned value management is just considered a part of the implementation phase, but it is such an important concept—and sometimes understanding the concept is difficult upon initial introduction to it—that a

EVM

chapter solely dedicated to earned value management seems appropriate. The reader should, therefore, consider Chapters 8 and 9 as one entity: the implementation phase.

IMPLEMENTING THE PROJECT

The project manager's next step after project approval is to put those things in motion that are required to start performing the work of the project. There are several steps that the project manager and the parent organization must go through in order to ensure that the project gets started according to the plan. Figure 8.1 shows the key steps in this process. These steps are planned during the development phase, but obviously cannot be acted on until the project manager and team receive the final approval to proceed. Note that many of the steps in Figure 8.1 are not sequential. They can be started in parallel. The primary consideration at this stage is to get the project under way as soon as possible while ensuring that each of the critical steps is accomplished.

Control Accounts

It generally is not too difficult to monitor and control a small project with one simple budget. The budget is used to track the project as a whole, and usually there is no compelling requirement to track the budget in greater detail than the third level of the work breakdown structure (WBS). In larger, more complex projects, however, this approach would not have enough

---

1. Set up control accounts
2. Colocate team
3. Design a monitoring system
4. Issue work orders
5. Contract with vendors
6. Issue request for proposal for competitive bids
7. Hire personnel
8. Train personnel

FIGURE 8.1.   Project Implementation Process

sensitivity to the nuances in performance that occur in multiple tasks or subtasks. Consequently, tracking project variances would be impossible. Specifically, project overruns could be detected but not the sources of the overruns.

To overcome this problem, the concept of *control accounts*—formally known as cost accounts—was developed. It involves breaking a project down into small elements and monitoring each of these elements individually. Each element has its own cost or budget associated with it, so that its progress can be measured directly against the planned budget.

In Chapter 3, the WBS and WBS dictionary were discussed in detail. To review, the term *dictionary* is used because it defines exactly what the work is and how it will be accomplished. The WBS dictionary for each work package provides at least the following information:

- A short but concise description of the work to be accomplished
- A schedule to begin and finish the work
- Who, by name, is responsible for accomplishing the work
- A list of labor resources, materials, and equipment needed to accomplish the task
- A budget for the task

All of these characteristics of the work package are elements of the control account, with the exception that the budget in a control account has to be time phased to be monitored. The budget for each individual task can be time phased in a Gantt chart or in a spreadsheet, such Microsoft Excel, to allow for a day-by-day assessment of expenditures against the plan.

Colocate the Project Team

The project team should be colocated if at all possible, if not in the same large room then on the same floor of a building and, ideally, in the same general section of a floor.

There are several reasons why colocating the team is beneficial:

- Working closely together on a project builds team spirit.
- Team morale is enhanced when team members feel that they are physically and mentally connected.
- It enhances good communication between the project manager and the team and among the team members.

■ Project problems often can be avoided when team members are close enough to discuss difficulties as they occur.

Although the ideal situation is for the team to be colocated, the reality is that most organizations do not have the space to colocate each project team. The next best alternative is to establish a "war room" for the team: a room set aside for the exclusive use of the project team. The room should be large enough for team meetings and to maintain files relevant to the project.

Design a Monitoring System

Setting up a monitoring system is crucial to the control process. Without a way to track and analyze each of the tasks of a project, it is not possible to make the decisions necessary to control the progress of a project. Many organizations have established standard procedures for monitoring projects. If this is not the case, it is incumbent upon the project manager and his or her team to do so. The monitoring process and procedures need to be documented and approved by all the stakeholders.

Issue Work Orders

In order for a project to begin, the project manager must issue the appropriate work orders. In addition to authorizing the work to begin, each work order is also a small but crucial part of the control process. A work order specifies how requirements are to be fulfilled, how much can be spent on a task, and how long the work should take.

Figure 8.2 is a sample work order/work order amendment form. As shown in the figure, every work order should include at least the following information:

■ Contract and work order/amendment number
■ Purpose
■ Statement of work
■ Deliverables and their due dates
■ Budget
■ Position of the task in the WBS
■ Signatures of person authorizing and person accepting responsibility

WORK ORDER/WORK ORDER AMENDMENT		
Project Manager:	**Contract No.:**	**Work Order No.:**
Task Leader:	**Amendment No.:**	**Date Issued:**

By signing below, the Project Manager and the Task Leader acknowledge that this Work Order is issued under the provisions of the primary contract shown above. The services authorized are within the scope of services set forth in the *Purpose* of this contract. All rights and obligations of the parties shall be subject to and governed by the terms and conditions. Amendment(s) (if applicable) and the signed Primary Agreement, including any subsequent modifications, are hereby incorporated by reference.

Purpose

(Attach additional sheets if necessary)

Statement of Work

Deliverables and Due Date:

Deliverables are subject to review and approval by
the Project Manager prior to acceptance of the work.
(Attach additional sheets if necessary)

Start Date	End Date

Budget

Description/Task	Quantity	Unit (Hrs)	Unit Cost	Total
1			$	$
2			$	$
Business Objective Supported:	Project budget shall pay an amount not to exceed			$

Both the Project Manager and the Task Leader are responsible for ensuring work performed is within the scope of this Work Order or Work Order Amendment. The Project Manager must monitor proper compliance with the terms of this Work Order and applicable statutes and regulations. **IN WITNESS WHEREOF, the parties have executed this Work Contract.**

Task Leader Approval		Project Manager Approval	
Signature	*Date*	*Signature*	*Date*
Print Name		Print Name	
Phone	E-mail	Phone	E-mail

FIGURE 8.2. Sample Work Order/Work Order Amendment Form

Contract with Vendors

There are very few projects that do not have some vendor-required items. Although most organizations have a procurement department that specializes in contracting with vendors, it remains the project manager's responsibility to initiate the request for purchase. It is also the project manager, or the designated technical representative, who provides the requisite specifications for the requested items. In some cases, though, in particular when the technical solution requires the services of a team member rather than the services of a vendor, the project manager is responsible for negotiating the teaming agreement.

Issue Request for Proposal for Competitive Bids

A request for proposal (RFP) formally invites contractors or vendors to bid on some part of a project. For instance, a project might require a specialized software program that a company cannot develop in-house. An RFP is then prepared, which describes the project's requirements and provides detailed specifications on which qualified companies can bid. RFPs are issued with very precise instructions about how, where, and when bidders should respond. The response to an RFP is a proposal that contains price and schedule estimates as well as a technical approach.

Hire Personnel

In many projects, the organizational strategy is to hire personnel to fill the specialized billets in the project organization. Although the human resources department is responsible for advertising to fill positions and administering the hiring procedures, the project manager generally has the final say on who is hired for the project. Hence, the project manager has to have a good understanding of interviewing techniques and procedures, as well as a thorough knowledge of the administrative processes, company benefits, and career potential with the organization.

Train Personnel

There may be a need to train some project personnel before they can begin work on a project. For instance, in a project to develop some specialized software using the customer's processes, procedures, or computer language, it may be necessary for the project manager to develop and schedule some special training courses.

MONITORING THE PROJECT

Three activities comprise the monitoring process: data collection, data analysis, and information reporting. The project manager's responsibility is to establish a process for collecting data (how data will be collected and how often) and set up a reporting hierarchy for disseminating the information after it is analyzed. To a very large degree, the reporting hierarchy will already be set as a part of the stakeholder analysis done early in the concept and planning phases. However, once a project gets under way, it is not unusual for people who have not previously shown any interest in it to emerge. A good way to ensure that the reporting hierarchy is correct and is approved is to prepare a reporting matrix like the one in Figure 8.3.

Data Collection

Sources of data vary, and the project manager must take advantage of every one of them. The average project manager will spend approximately 90% of his or her time communicating with the project team, senior management, the customer, and other stakeholders. The majority of this time is spent either collecting or transmitting data.

Data collection does not have to follow a formal process. In fact, most project data are gathered informally. However, data sent from the project office are most often presented formally through a status report or status briefing.

Data Analysis

Collecting data is only half of the challenge; analyzing the data is the second half. Because the project manager spends so much time communicating with the project team, it is often the case that he or she is provided with so much information that it is not possible to process it all.

Analyzing data is a necessary step in the process because data alone do not show impact on a project. Before any information is sent by the project

Data Item	Report Description	Project Manager	Senior Manager	Director of Software Development	Director of Contracts	Director of Finance	Customer Project Manager				
	Data Item Distribution										
1	Status reports (monthly)	x	x	x	x		x				
2	Status reports (weekly)	x									
3	Monthly financial reports	x	x			x					
4	Configuration change reports	x		x							
5	Manpower utilization reports	x		x							
6	Exception reports	x	x								
7	Variance reports	x	x			x					
8											
9											
10											

FIGURE 8.3. Sample Reporting Matrix

team, there has to be an accurate assessment of the impact and a proposed solution for correcting any problems that might exist.

Most project data of concern involve the budget, the schedule, or the performance or quality of a project. Among the tools for analyzing the data relative to these three project characteristics, earned value is being used more and more for analyzing budget and schedule impacts. (Refer to Chapter 9 for a detailed discussion of earned value and how to apply it.)

Information Reporting

Information reporting is done either through formal reports, such as status reports, or through informational briefings. The project manager or project team uses several different types of reports. All these reports can be classified as status reports in a broad sense, but generally the term *status report* is used to refer to those that routinely describe the progress of a project. Other types of reports detail problems or provide specialized information such as financial deviations or changes to the project baseline.

Status Reports

A status report is a narrative description of the progress of a project, usually provided to senior management and the customer representative on a regular basis, say each month. The frequency of a status report, or any other report, usually is a function of how complex or risky a project is. For instance, a project that involves new technology with significant financial consequences for the contractor or the customer would likely require frequent— even daily—informal status reporting, with formal reports due weekly or biweekly.

The type of information required in a status report varies from organization to organization. The basic information required in a status report is shown in Figure 8.4. Some organizations opt for more detailed status reports rather than several different reports for specialized reasons.

Variance Reports

Variances are deviations from the planned budget or schedule. Many customers, particularly external customers, require variance reports. The typical variance report will have a line graph showing the cumulative budget and schedule plotted against the actual budget and schedule. Any variances (positive if below budget or ahead of schedule and negative if over budget or behind schedule) have to be explained. If a project is over budget or behind schedule, the variance report will also have to reflect the plan to correct the problem.

Exception Reports

Exception reporting is a part of *exception management*—how senior managers will handle the situation when something out of the ordinary happens. For instance, the project manager's functional supervisor, or another senior executive, may impose some limit on a key project element, usually the budget, above or below which he or she has to be informed. For example, as long as actual expenditures are within, say, 10% of the budget, the project manager is responsible for correcting the variances. If the budget exceeds the

---

STATUS REPORT

Project Name: Report Date:

Project Phase: Report Period:

Project Manager:

Summary of Progress for Period:

Problems Encountered and Action Taken:

Planned Activities for Next Reporting Period:

Anticipated Problems:

Recommendations:

FIGURE 8.4. Sample Status Report Form

10% limit, whether over or under, then the project manager is obligated to issue an exception report to the appropriate manager for action.

CONTROLLING THE PROJECT

To control a project generally means controlling four things:

1. Cost variances
2. Schedule variances
3. Scope changes
4. Risk

Cost Variances

Cost variances are deviations of actual expenditures from the project budget. Variances occur in every project because it is virtually impossible to predict with 100% accuracy what will happen once a project is under way. Controlling these deviations from the budget is a major problem in most projects. Sometimes budget problems arise simply because the organization or project manager accepted a bid that was too low, but the biggest problems arise from inaccurate cost estimating.

Schedule Variances

Schedule variances usually occur because of unreasonable schedule constraints. Generally, the project team can estimate the actual duration requirements with reasonable accuracy, and if not, the PERT method provides a means for determining reasonable task duration. The problem is not so much an inability to estimate the schedule but rather the imposition of a schedule that is too tight.

Most projects are initiated to meet specific needs, such as critical training, improvement of existing systems, or competitive challenges. In most cases, these projects are reactive responses to a requirement and therefore start later than they should. If a project is responding to a critical need, then there is always a sense of urgency, causing the completion date to be set unreasonably early. The late start and early completion create a compressed schedule that is almost never achievable.

If the cost or schedule variances become too large, the project plan will have to be rewritten, the schedule revised, or the end-item product redesigned.

Scope Changes

Changes to the project baseline are inevitable. They are caused by several different factors, including inaccurate budget and schedule estimates; government health, safety, or environmental standards mandates; and changes recommended by the customer or project team as project knowledge grows. Change in a project is controlled through a configuration management process. This is a formal process designed by the project manager and team, or in some cases is an in-place organizational process, to screen recommended changes, track approved changes, and update the development process.

1. **Screening recommended changes**—Changes to a project can be recommended by the customer as well as team members and other functional groups. These recommendations should be directed to the project manager, who will assess the impacts of the changes on the project. Many organizations have a change control board (CCB) to deal with this kind of change. CCBs are routinely found in engineering organizations, where project changes have significant technical impact. Membership on a CCB consists of three to five persons representative of a company's technical expertise. CCB meetings are usually scheduled or called rather regularly, since project changes require quick decisions, and waiting for the next CCB meeting could affect the project schedule. If a CCB does not exist, the project manager should form one because every project, especially complex ones, will have a large number of requests that need to be handled expeditiously. Some of the requested changes will have no effect on the project budget, schedule, or resources, and the project manager usually is authorized to approve these changes unilaterally. However, any change that does impact the project budget, schedule, or resources should be approved only by a higher authority or a CCB.
2. **Tracking approved changes**—Once a change is approved, the project manager's designated configuration management special-

ist must document the change and update the project specifications. In large contracts, the configuration management process is
very elaborate and very detailed, with each change documented,
numbered with a configuration item number, and logged. The
configuration management position is so important that it has
become a separate labor category and is considered to be a spe-
cialist function.

3. **Updating the development process**—After a change is approved
   and the files are updated, the project baseline is updated, the changes
   are published, and all stakeholders are informed of the change.

Changes to the baseline often—in fact, usually—require a change to the
contract. No project change should ever be approved without an attendant
change to the contract. Even if the customer decides to change the baseline
configuration and it is determined that there is no impact on the budget or
schedule, a no-cost contract modification should be requested by the project
manager. Usually the customer will automatically issue one, but the experienced project manager will always insist upon having a contract modification prior to instituting a change. These contract modifications are necessary because one of the actions at project completion is to determine
whether the goals, objectives, and specifications have been met. Without a
contract modification, there is no way to track whether or why a change was
made.

Risk

Although this book has not discussed risk in any detail, it is worth reviewing
the basic tenets of risk management, which is an ongoing process, at this
point because risk is most prevalent—or damaging—during the implementation phase of a project.

The life of a project manager is a life of conflict. In truth, project management is conflict management. The project manager's job is to smoothly
negotiate the obstacles encountered during every phase in the life of a project.
If there were no risk or conflict in a project, there would be no need for a
project manager; project management would become an administr͘͘͘

Risk is two-sided: there is the possibility of loss and the
Project risks can exhibit extremes on both sides. The

a risk event occurs unabated, but the gains can be immense if a risk is planned for and eliminated or at least mitigated and made manageable.

Risk Defined

Risk is characterized by three components:

- **The event**—What can happen to the project, good or bad?
- **Probability of event occurrence**—What is the chance the event will happen?
- **Impact to the project**—What is the effect on the project, good or bad, if the event actually does occur?

Types of Risk

There are two types of risk: business and pure, or insurable, risk. Risk is not necessarily negative; it may be an opportunity for gain. The key to risk management is to recognize the potential risk events and whether they can be directed and controlled for a neutral or positive effect on the project. If a risk event can only lead to negative impacts, then it should not be attempted; it should be avoided or transferred to someone else or to another organization.

Business Risks

A business risk provides an opportunity for gain as well as for loss. An example of a business risk is a customer change to the project scope. The change might represent a risk to the provider because it involves skills or expertise the company does not possess. However, the scope change might produce additional revenue if the company can hire additional resources, team with another company, or hire a vendor to provide the necessary expertise.

Business risks are the risks that are managed. Management of insurable, or pure, risks should never be attempted.

Insurable or Pure Risks

Insurable risks, sometimes called pure risks because they offer only opportunities for loss, are risks that an organization should never take on. Incredibly, software development groups routinely attempt such projects because of the prevailing view that everything can be fixed with software.

Examples of insurable risks are natural disasters, such as a fire, flood, hurricane, and earthquake. For instance, if a company is located in a high-risk area for hurricanes, it will insure against such loss. But there are other, more subtle types of pure risk.

Often, a company will attempt a project because the major project requirements are within its capability, even though one or two other requirements may not be. The thinking is that since the company is qualified to accomplish the majority of the project requirements, it will be able to complete the rest. Mature, or learning, organizations recognize these disastrous situations and plan for them. These organizations have effective project selection and risk management processes.

The risk management process is best understood by considering a risk management model such as the one in the next section. This risk management model can be applied in any organization and in any industry.

A Risk Management Model

Risk management, like every critical management activity, is best accomplished when a formalized and documented set of guidelines and standard operating procedures are implemented and followed by everyone in the company. The Project Management Institute (PMI®) has provided guidelines for a risk management process in its *Guide to the Project Management Body of Knowledge* (*PMBOK® Guide*)* as well as its own model. The model in Figure 8.5 contains all the PMI® model steps but is more detailed to better explain the risk management components and process elements.

One key component of the PMI® model that is implicit, but not stated, is continual evaluation. Risk management is an ongoing process that continues throughout the life cycle of a project.

Sections of the Risk Management Plan

The risk management plan provides guidance in the process of managing the risks of a particular project. Therefore, it is imperative that a plan is devel-

---

* *A Guide to the Project Management Body of Knowledge,* 3rd ed. South Darby, Pa.: PMI, 2004.

Document and communicate every step

Step 1. Planning Risk Management
Step 2. Identify and Assess Risk
Step 3. Qualify Risk
Step 4. Quantify Risk
Step 5. Develop and Implement Risk Response
Step 6. Track Risk Response
Step 7. Control Risk
Step 8. Document and Archive Risk History

FIGURE 8.5. Risk Management Model

oped for every project and that the plan clearly identifies how the project risks will be identified, responded to, tracked, and controlled.

The generic risk management plan in Figure 8.6 has nine sections:

1. **Project name and brief scope description**—This section provides the name of the project (and often the project manager's name) as well as a short description of the purpose of the project.
2. **Risk management methodology**—This section provides narrative about the tools or techniques used to identify the risks and how

---

RISK MANAGEMENT PLAN

    I. Project Name and Brief Scope Description
   II. Risk Management Methodology
  III. Roles and Responsibilities
  IV. Funding
   V. Risk Measurement and Interpretation Methodology
  VI. Levels of Risk Response Responsibility
 VII. Risk Communication Plan
VIII. Risk Tracking and Documentation
  IX. Appendices
     A. Risk Table
     B. Risk Response Plan

FIGURE 8.6. Risk Management Plan Format

the risk response strategies will be determined. It also contains the data sources from which the risks and risk strategies are developed, such as historical data from previous similar projects.

3. **Roles and responsibilities**—The roles and responsibilities of each project team member and other task contributors should be clearly defined in this section. If responsibility to report, eliminate, or track a risk is not clearly assigned, a usually diligent team member can easily ignore an impending risk event. Of course, the project manager has ultimate responsibility for administering the risk plan and risk response strategies, but he or she can, and should, delegate responsibility for identifying risks and reporting triggers that presage a risk event.

4. **Funding**—Budgets for risk contingencies should be defined and guidance for their administration published at the start of a project. Many organizations assign responsibility for the contingency, or reserve funding, pool to the project manager. However, funding for contingencies is strictly the responsibility of senior management in other organizations. This section of the risk management plan should clearly state how the contingency funding is to be administered.

5. **Risk measurement and interpretation methodology**—The method or methods used to measure risk and how the scores are interpreted are defined in this section. Most companies have guidelines for applying a weighting factor and/or a score for each type of risk. Scoring methods are important in both the quantitative and qualitative analyses to reduce the effects of subjectively assigning a value to a risk. Scoring methods should be chosen in advance, and they should be applied consistently throughout all steps of the risk management process.

6. **Levels of risk response responsibility**—This section defines who has responsibility for each risk response according to a predetermined threshold. That is, during a project life cycle, risk events of different levels of impact can occur. The project manager has discretionary authority to handle certain levels of risk, but he or she must elevate the decision to a higher senior management position or to a committee if the impact of a risk exceeds a certain monetary level. In some instances, only the customer has the authority to implement certain risk response strategies because of

the cost to the project in time and money. The effectiveness of a risk management plan is measured against how well any actual risk event is kept below the lowest risk threshold.

7. **Risk communication plan**—This section describes report formats and outlines who receives reports of risk events, responses implemented, and the effectiveness of the risk response strategies.

8. **Risk tracking and documentation**—This section describes the process for tracking the effectiveness of the risk response strategies and how they are documented and archived as lessons learned.

9. **Appendices**—This section provides a vehicle for attaching any additional information or plans, depending upon the needs of each individual project. The two most common appendices are the risk table and the risk response plan.

   - **Risk table**—A table or matrix of all the identified risks in a project. Many project teams prefer that the table contain only those risks being managed at the moment and that it be changed or revised as each risk is dealt with.

   - **Risk response plan**—A detailed plan that explains the response strategies for each of the identified risks in the risk table.

Every lessons learned analysis should be documented and archived, with easy access to the information by all project managers and teams. Many companies have begun making these lessons learned libraries available online to make them even more accessible and effective. But even a hard copy in an organization's resource library is far better than no access at all. Many projects have been saved the problems and costs of reinventing the wheel by having access to workable solutions for risks that continue to reoccur.

SUMMARY

The implementation phase of a project life cycle involves starting the project, monitoring its progress, and controlling day-to-day activities so that variances from the project plan are kept to a minimum.

The key to success in this phase is monitoring the system design. If the project manager and team put into place a systematic way to collect data, analyze the data, control the variances revealed in the analyses, and report the results quickly, then the project will progress smoothly. Otherwise, the project will be characterized by constant, reactive attempts to put out fires.

Another key aspect of project success revolves around the expertise and efficiency of the team in risk management. Amazingly, a very large segment of the corporate world does not engage in any formalized risk-planning process. Not to do so is to invite disaster.

The key tools for this phase of a project are the WBS, Gantt charts, network analyses, earned value analyses, statistical analyses, and various report formats.

MONITORING
AND CONTROL

Earned value management has been in use as a means for measuring—that is, monitoring and controlling—project progress since 1968. Prior to that time, tracking project progress essentially consisted of monitoring the actual cost against the budget and the actual schedule against the estimate, but no method was available that assessed the combined impacts of costs and schedule. Nor were there any standards for analyzing and reporting these data until the Department of Defense (DOD) developed instructions to its contractors for:

- Developing work breakdown structures
- Developing certain key planning elements such as baselines
- Defining cost allocations and procedures for collecting and reporting cost data
- Analyzing budget and schedule variances and predicting future project costs
- Preparing performance reports

One of the most beneficial components of this DOD instruction is the method of project progress analysis known as earned value. Only the DOD and its contractors used this method until the late 1980s or early 1990s, when the private sector began to adopt it as the analysis tool of choice. The method can be used on small and large projects and is independent of the type of contract used to execute a project.

The concept of earned value is sometimes difficult to grasp, though not because the concept or the procedure is difficult. The problem is basically twofold: earned value has a language of its own and schedule is measured in terms of dollars instead of time. Since measuring schedule in this fashion goes against intuition and experience, some people focus on the language rather than on the concepts of earned value. The result is that learning earned value analysis techniques is harder than it should be.

The key to understanding earned value is in understanding three terms:

1. Budgeted cost of work scheduled or the planned value of work
2. Actual cost of work performed
3. Budgeted cost of work actually performed or the "earned" value

Once these terms and the concepts they represent are mastered, all the other terms and components of earned value analysis are easy to remember and use. This chapter explains earned value and demonstrates how it is used to track a task or the progress of a project. But first, just what do evaluation and control mean?

UNDERSTANDING EVALUATION AND CONTROL IN PROJECT MANAGEMENT

Evaluation is an official examination and verification of project progress, status, and financial health, according to the *PMBOK® Guide*. It is official as opposed to casual. In other words, the evaluation is done as a requirement of the project manager's or project team's responsibility for determining the progress of a project, and it is usually done as a part of the status review and reporting process. It is official too, because it has the weight of the project manager's organization and the customer's organization behind it. In fact, evaluations can be official because the customer requires them by contract.

Control is paired with evaluation because control is the process of comparing actual project performance with planned performance. Control also involves analyzing these performance data to determine whether some corrective action is appropriate. One major tool used to determine if a process is in- or out-of-control tolerance is the *control chart*, which can be constructed around many different parameters. Control charts are widely used to track quality measures, but they can be equally effective for tracking other project data as well. Some uses of control charts are discussed and demonstrated later in this chapter.

An important aspect of control in project management is that it is done on a regular basis, in fact daily, whereas evaluation is more of a big-picture perspective. Evaluation looks at the whole project context, whereas control is the day-by-day assessment of how resources, tasks, and elements of the work breakdown structure are doing. Another consideration is that control is only at the micro level, whereas evaluation is at the macro level. Finally, a good thing about a control action or project monitoring is that it is relatively cheap.

CONTROLLING SCHEDULE AND COST

In its simplest form, schedule and cost control means:

- Comparing planned and actual project progress and costs
- Determining a strategy for limiting variation from the schedule and cost baselines
- Managing the activities required to maintain the schedule and costs within acceptable limits

"Acceptable limits" is a relative term because some organizations set very tight limits within which a project must progress and other organizations are less stringent. One thing to bear in mind, though, is that studies show that a project that gets as much as 15% or greater away from either the schedule or cost baseline can never be recovered to closer than 10% of the original plan. In other words, a limit of about 10% away from the baseline should be the corridor within which a project manager works to maintain control of a project.

Performance Control Charts

Performance control charts come in many forms, but the most common and most useful for schedule and cost control is the one shown in Figure 9.1. The chart has three curves. The middle curve in the graphic is the cumulative cost

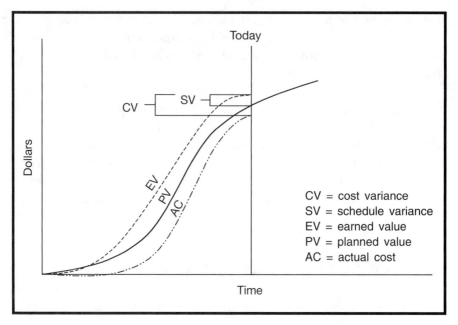

FIGURE 9.1.   Earned Value Management Key Curve Components

curve for the entire project. It is the estimated cost of all the tasks summed to represent the expected cost over the life of the project. The very top end of this curve, if measured against the dollars axis, is the budget at completion or the total cost of the project. The bottom curve in the graphic is a plot of the actual costs spent over time.

These two curves were, before the advent of earned value, all that was used to measure how a project was doing against the plan. It is interesting to note that if only these two curves are used, one would immediately assume that the project is under budget and doing quite nicely.

The problem is, the information from these two curves does not tell anything about how the project is doing against the schedule. That information is provided by the third curve, which plots the earned value or actual work accomplished against the plan.

The project shown in Figure 9.1 is in fact doing very well; the project is under budget and ahead of schedule—but without the earned value curve data, one really wouldn't know that.

WHAT IS EARNED VALUE MANAGEMENT?

As mentioned at the beginning of this chapter, earned value was developed when the DOD set guidelines for its contractors to collect, analyze, and present financial and progress data. Earned value management has been in use for over 40 years in the federal sector but was only embraced by the private sector in the late 1980s and early 1990s. The Project Management Institute deserves much of the credit for "legitimizing" earned value management in the private sector because it recognized its major benefits in tracking and controlling project performance early and pushed its use in the project management world. Earned value management now is recognized worldwide and in every industry as the most accurate monitoring and controlling technique.

What exactly is earned value management? Simply put, it is a way to integrate scope, schedule, and resources as a tool to measure project progress. Since it provides a standard way of calculating progress, it is a consistent measurement across an organization and across industries. The great advantage provided by earned value management is that now schedule can be measured against planned progress, and it offers a way to compare planned costs, actual costs, and schedule progress in the same graph. This is a major benefit because now if actual spending, say, exceeds the budget, an evaluation of the actual progress made might show the project is ahead of schedule.

It spite of its wide acceptance, some project managers and organizations view earned value as an administrative burden that is not worth the time it takes to calculate it. The truth is, however, that it is easy to set up, is already a part of project management software, and provides such an accurate measure of performance progress that one really cannot afford not to use it.

To use earned value management, though, requires learning a new set of jargon. Some of the jargon is not completely new; it is just used in a slightly different way than you might be familiar with.

KEY EARNED VALUE TERMINOLOGY

There are three earned value terms that have to be understood before using earned value analysis:

- Planned value
- Actual cost
- Earned value

If someone has a problem understanding earned value, it is usually because the concept behind these three terms is not clearly understood. Because of the importance of these three terms in understanding the concept of earned value, we will discuss them in some detail.

Planned Value

Planned value (PV) is the sum of approved cost estimates scheduled to be performed during a task life, project life, or any given time period during the duration of a project. In simple terms, it is the estimated cost of all the tasks of a project, and it is traditionally shown as a cumulative cost curve. It is not new information for project planning and control; it is simply called by a different name.

Actual Cost

Actual cost (AC) is the amount of money actually expended during a task or project performance. It is the amount paid for labor, materials, and all other direct costs. This also is not a new concept; it is simply the actual project costs or actuals.

So far, nothing new has been discussed; just new terminology has been introduced. The comparison of these two curves, budget and actuals, has traditionally been used to measure project performance. But again, the major problem here is that data from these curves alone do not say anything about the schedule progress. The real breakthrough came with the introduction of the concept of "earned value." The concept of earned value is not new in terms of time, but rather is new to many organizations and project teams.

Earned Value

Earned value (EV) is the sum of the estimated costs of those tasks or parts of tasks that have actually been completed. The concept is a little hard to understand at first because it is new and because it is difficult to grasp a concept that uses an estimated cost and actual completed work in the same breath—they seem contradictory. Perhaps looking at it from the perspective of a firm fixed-price contract might help clarify the concept.

Relationship of Earned Value and Planned Value

Consider a small project that is estimated to last five months. For the sake of convenience and explanation, assume the project is made up of five sequential tasks, each one month long and each requiring the same amount of effort. In negotiating with the customer for some sort of progress payment agreement, the customer agrees to pay at the end of every month provided the task for that period is completed. For each month, then, the plan is to complete 20% of the project.

If the total project estimated cost is $1,000, then at the end of the first month the plan is to complete 20% of the project and to spend $200 (0.20 × $1,000). This is the PV for this reporting period. If the task is completed on time, then the customer will pay the $200 because it was *earned* by completing the planned work for that period. Thus the EV is also $200.

Suppose at the end of the second month, when the project manager asks the customer for the progress payment, only 10% of the second task has been finished. The project manager *planned* to have completed 40% of the total project by this point and to spend $400, but has only completed 30% of the planned work. Thus the total PV at the end of the second month is $400, but the project manager has only *earned* 0.30 × $1,000 = $300. Therefore, at the second reporting period, the PV = $400 and the EV = $300.

To look at it another way, PV is the cumulative estimated expenditure for a task or a project at a given time during its life cycle. The EV is the amount of the estimated cost that represents the work that is *actually* completed during that same time period. If a $1,000 task were evaluated at the 50% mark in its life, one would expect the expenditures (or PV) to be $500 at that point. If the task is only 40% complete, then the EV is $400; if 60% complete, then the EV is $600. This can be expressed as a mathematical formula:

$$EV = \% \text{ complete} \times PV$$

Relationship of Earned Value and Actual Cost

Another point of confusion for some is *AC* versus EV. AC has absolutely nothing to do with EV or, for that matter, PV. AC is what is actually spent for the work done, that is, labor, materials, and so on. EV is an estimated value of the work actually done compared with the work planned.

If these three terms—AC, PV, and EV—and the concept behind the EV term are clearly understood, then the rest of the terms and most of the calculations are relatively easy and straightforward.

Other Key Earned Value Terms

The most important earned value terms, in addition to the three just discussed, are:

- **Budget at completion**—The cumulative cost for the total project. The budget at completion is the rolled-up or total cost of a project and represents the total expected expenditure for all the work at project completion.
- **Cost variance**—The difference between the estimated value of the work completed (that is, EV) and what is actually paid out for that work (that is, AC).
- **Schedule variance**—The difference between the estimated value of the work actually completed (EV) and the planned value completed (PV). Notice that the schedule variance is expressed in dollars. Using earned value, one can measure schedule progress in terms of dollars because work completed is defined with a dollar amount. The amount of time a project is ahead of or behind schedule can be read directly off the time axis of the cost graph.
- **Percent complete**—The amount of work completed to date compared with the planned work for the entire activity, whether a task(s) or a project.
- **Cost performance index**—Performance on the money spent. In other words, the cost performance index provides a look at how well a project is doing, measured by comparing the amount of work completed against the amount of work planned for completion during the same period. It can be thought of as the value of the work completed per each dollar *actually* spent.
- **Schedule performance index**—Performance on the money planned to be spent. The schedule performance index provides a look at how well the schedule is doing against how much was

planned for completion. It can be thought of as the value of work completed per each dollar *planned* to be spent.

With a working vocabulary, the techniques of earned value calculation and analysis can be examined.

APPLYING EARNED VALUE: AN EXAMPLE

The best way to understand the earned value calculations and analysis techniques is with an example. Consider the simple example in Figure 9.2.

This is a very simple project that has three tasks and will run for nine months. First, determine what the three key earned value components are. That is, what are PV, EV, and AC?

In this example, actual money spent for task A is $495, for task B is $225, and for task C is $350. The easiest way to determine and record these data is to use a table such as the one in Figure 9.3.

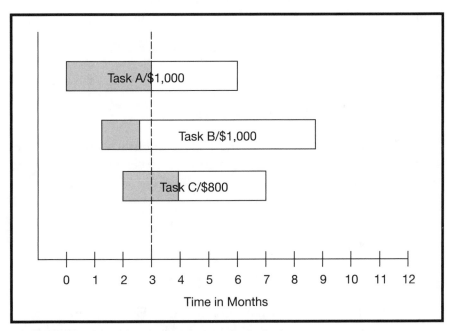

FIGURE 9.2. Applying Earned Value Analysis

Task	Task Cost Estimate	Actual % Complete	Planned % Complete	PV	EV	AC
A	$1,000	50	50	$500	$500	$495
B	$1,000	20	25	$250	$200	$225
C	$800	40	20	$160	$320	$350
Total	$2,800			$910	$1,020	$1,070

FIGURE 9.3. Earned Value Analysis Table

For the sake of convenience, assume the spending across each task is linear, although in reality it seldom is. The costs for the tasks would have to be estimated on a week-by-week basis for the calculations to be completely accurate, but an assumption of linearity is not bad unless relatively large spending spikes are anticipated.

To determine the PV for each task, look at the time of the data point and determine what percentage completion is expected. These estimates are shown in the fourth column of Figure 9.3, and PV is calculated by:

$$PV = \text{Planned \% complete} \times \text{Task cost estimate}$$

For the example:

$$PV = 0.50 \times \$1,000 = \$500$$

To calculate the EV, determine the percentage of the work that has actually been completed, shown by the shaded area in Figure 9.2 and recorded in the third column of Figure 9.3. The value for EV is calculated by:

$$EV = \text{Actual \% complete} \times \text{Task cost estimate}$$

For example, for task B:

$$EV = 0.20 \times \$1,000 = \$200$$

The totals for the PV, EV, and AC columns in Figure 9.3 are the totals up to that point in time. With this basic information, the earned value analysis can be done.

EARNED VALUE ANALYSIS: FORMULAS AND THEIR INTERPRETATION

Variance Indicators

Variance indicators are the most used and most useful project performance measures. This is so because they are measures that closely resemble those traditionally used and those that senior management looks for.

There are two variance indicators: cost variance and schedule variance. Both are calculated numbers using the three data values previously determined: PV, EV, and AC.

Cost Variance

Cost variance (CV) is the difference between the value of the work actually completed and the amount of money actually spent for the work. CV is calculated by the formula:

$$CV = EV - AC$$

Using the data in Figure 9.3 for the example:

$$CV = \$1,020 - \$1,070$$
$$= -\$50$$

The negative figure indicates the project is over budget. A positive value would indicate the project is under budget, and 0 would indicate it is exactly on budget.

Schedule Variance

Schedule variance (SV) is the difference between the value of the work actually completed and the amount estimated for the work. SV is calculated by:

$$SV = EV - PV$$

Again, using the data in Figure 9.3 for the example:

$$SV = \$1,020 - \$910$$
$$= \$110$$

Thus, for this example, at the time of the data sample or reporting date, the project is over budget, but it is ahead of schedule as indicated by a positive SV. A negative value would indicate the project is behind schedule, and 0 would indicate it is on schedule.

Performance Indices

The variance measurements are wonderful indicators for the project manager or the project team, but senior management, and particularly those in finance, generally can relate better to an index that shows performance relative to actual expenditures or planned progress. Thus the cost and schedule performance indices are especially good for communicating progress to these stakeholders. Fortunately for us, the performance indices are calculated using the same numbers we used for the variances.

Cost Performance Index

The cost performance index (CPI) is calculated by dividing the value of the work actually performed by the AC of the work:

$$CPI = EV/AC$$
$$= \$1,020/\$1,070$$
$$= 0.95$$

This number is interpreted to mean that for every dollar spent on the work, the return is only 95 cents value in value. A CPI less than 1 means that spending is more than is being returned in value, a CPI greater than 1 means that the project is worth more than is being spent, and a CPI of 1 means the project is exactly on budget.

CPI is a practical forecasting tool because it can be plotted and trends determined from the data. Many project managers develop a control chart layout for the CPI data and use it as a control mechanism by maintaining the CPI curve within a preagreed-upon upper and lower control limit, much as is done with quality control charts and their upper and lower standard deviation lines.

Schedule Performance Index

The schedule performance index (SPI) is calculated by dividing the value of the work actually performed by the planned cost of the work:

$$SPI = EV/PV$$
$$= \$1{,}020/\$910$$
$$= 1.12$$

This index value is interpreted as showing how well the actual performance of the project is doing against the plan. If the SPI is greater than 1, then the project is ahead of schedule; less than 1, it is behind schedule; and equal to 1, it is on schedule.

These indices show that although the example project is over budget, it is ahead of schedule.

Percent Complete and Percent Spent

These two percent calculations, and the completion estimates in the next section, are especially important for communicating project performance to the stakeholders. Almost all status or progress reports require these calculations because of their importance to the overall organizational health and because of future planning ramifications.

Percent complete (PC) is calculated by dividing the value of the actual work performed (EV) by the project budget at completion (BAC) or by the latest revised estimate at completion, which will be discussed shortly. The PC is calculated by:

$$PC = EV/BAC$$

For the example:

$$PC = \$1{,}020/\$2{,}800$$
$$= 0.36$$

The example project is a little over 36% complete.

The percent spent (PS) is calculated by dividing the actual expenditures to date by the BAC:

$$PS = AC/BAC$$
$$= \$1,070/\$2,800$$
$$= 0.38$$

This means that 38% of the budget has been spent.

These calculations are important for communicating with the stakeholders, but they are also very important to the project manager because he or she needs to be able to judge whether there is enough left in the budget to finish the project.

Completion Estimates

These calculations are made to determine how a project is doing compared to the plan and how close the plan is likely to be to the original projections. There are three key completion estimates needed by the project team and by senior management: the estimate at completion, the variance at completion, and the estimate to complete. Another often asked for completion estimate is the to-complete performance index.

Estimate at Completion

Estimate at completion (EAC) is a new estimate of how much a project is going to cost. As a project progresses, data improve and estimates for the baseline become more accurate. Since the baseline is an estimate to begin with, it is important to determine how good the estimate was and whether the budget, or schedule, needs to be refined.

Every time data are analyzed (that is, an evaluation milestone is reached), a new EAC is calculated by dividing the BAC (for the first evaluation) or the latest EAC (for subsequent evaluations) by the CPI:

$$EAC = BAC \text{ (or latest EAC)}/CPI$$

Using the BAC from the example data in Figure 9.3 and the calculated CPI, the new EAC is calculated:

$$EAC = \$2,800/0.95$$
$$= \$2,947.37$$

The new EAC is greater than the original estimate, and a decision has to be made as to whether and how the project can be brought back to the budget line.

Variance at Completion

Variance at completion (VAC) is the difference between the original estimate and the new EAC for a project. It is calculated by:

$$VAC = BAC - EAC$$

For the example:

$$VAC = \$2,800 - \$2,947.37$$
$$= -\$147.37$$

The variance is nearly $150, which means an additional $150 is needed if the project continues on this trend.

Is this amount of variance significant? It represents about 5% of the budget, and it certainly is serious enough to apply some correction strategies to keep the deficit from increasing. It is also serious enough that senior management needs to be informed about the projected increase, what caused it, and what is being done about it.

Estimate to Complete

Estimate to complete (ETC) is an estimate of how much more money is needed to run a project from the present date until completion. The ETC is particularly important to the comptroller or other financial officers in an organization because it is the number they will use to plan future cash flows. Also, it is the number that includes the potential budget increase and therefore is the basis for replanning the budget, if required.

The ETC is calculated by simply comparing the latest EAC to the amount of money actually expended to date:

$$ETC = EAC - AC$$

For the example:

$$ETC = \$2,947.37 - \$1,070$$
$$= \$1,877.37$$

The example project will need nearly $1,900 to pay for all the remaining work.

To-Complete Performance Index

The to-complete performance index (TCPI) is an estimate that provides the project manager and his or her team with an indication of how much effort will be required to get the project back on track or how likely it is that the project will get back on track. In other words, it provides an indicator of performance improvement needed to correct the project performance deficiencies.

The TCPI is a comparison of the work remaining to the budget remaining. The formula for this calculation is:

$$TCPI = (BAC - EV)/(BAC - AC)$$

Once again, using the example project:

$$TCPI = (\$2,947.37 - \$1,020)/(\$2,947.37 - \$1,070)$$
$$= \$1,927.37/\$1,877.37$$
$$= \$1.03$$

This TCPI is not so bad! If the project manager can change project management processes, motivate the team members to improve their performance, and/or correct problems in the project work, raising the performance level to make $1.03 on the dollar is certainly realistic. If, however, the TCPI were, say, 1.10 and performance was already below 1, the performance level (that is, meeting customer product requirements) would probably not be achievable unless the schedule was lengthened substantially, which would also increase the project costs.

Data Presentation

Calculations are fine and necessary, but what do they all mean? That is, how can they be portrayed so that these various elements of schedule and cost

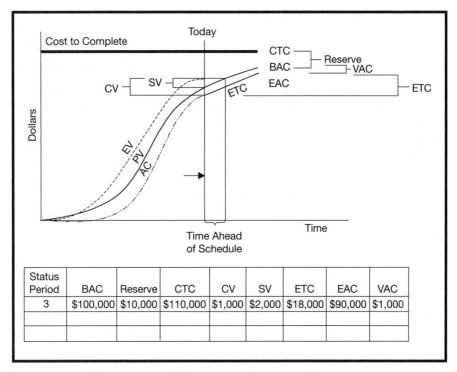

FIGURE 9.4. Earned Value Management Components

Status Period	BAC	Reserve	CTC	CV	SV	ETC	EAC	VAC
3	$100,000	$10,000	$110,000	$1,000	$2,000	$18,000	$90,000	$1,000

control can be viewed relative to each other? Figure 9.4 shows each of the key measures.

One additional financial term is indicated in Figure 9.4: the cost to complete (CTC). As shown in the figure, CTC is the BAC plus reserve. CTC is not as commonly used as the other terms because project managers either include the reserve in the project estimate if they have that control or senior management holds out the reserve for use if necessary. Either way, CTC usually is not figured into the operating budget for a project.

The tabular form of the earned value analysis is also shown in Figure 9.4 because a project manager most likely will be required to use both the graphic and tabular representations for analysis and for communication with stakeholders. It is easier to highlight and explain to stakeholders what the tabular data mean. Unless stakeholders are very familiar with earned value, the curves would have less meaning than the tabular information.

ESTIMATING PERCENT COMPLETE

The most difficult part of earned value analysis is estimating the percent complete a task is with any real accuracy. For a project that consists of making parts, building chairs, or anything else that can be counted, estimating percent complete is easy. For example, for a project to install 100 linear feet of fence in five days, it is obvious that 20 feet of fence has to be installed per day. At the end of each day, percentage complete for the total project can be calculated easily. But for a project that involves writing code, for example, or that requires design and development, estimating percent complete of such tasks is not so easy. The DOD long ago suggested to its contractors a way to simplify the percentage complete problem. It is called the 50-50 rule.

The 50-50 Rule

The difficulty in estimating percent complete with any degree of accuracy is well understood by anyone who has tried to do so. For the most part, these estimates are very subjective at best and usually optimistic. For those projects that use outside vendors or contractors, it is difficult, if not impossible, to get them to provide reliable evaluations of their work complete.

This situation was exactly the catalyst that made the DOD require its contractors to use the 50-50 rule when making to-complete projections. Using this method to determine percent complete ensures system integrity, it provides some consistency across organizations and across a project regardless of how many contractors are working on it, and it removes the subjectivity of "guessing" what the percent complete is.

How does it work? Actually, it is quite simple. Under the 50-50 rule, a task is considered to be 50% complete the instant work is begun, and it remains at 50% complete until all work on it is finished. Even though the actual percent complete of a task may be 10%, it is considered to be 50% complete for calculating PV and EV.

There are some obvious inaccuracies in this method of estimating completeness, and they would be significant for a small project that has few tasks. However, the method is actually very accurate when averaged over a number of tasks, particularly if all the tasks are approximately the same in length.

A simple example of the 50-50 rule will help clarify the method. For the sake of comparison, the example used earlier in defining the earned value terms and calculations will be used for the 50-50 rule (see Figure 9.5).

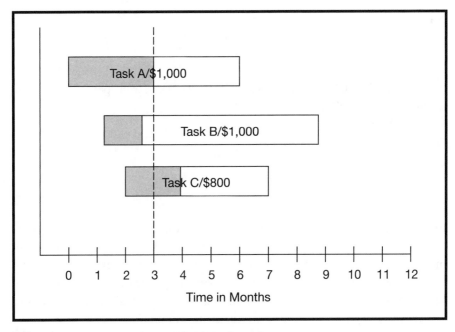

FIGURE 9.5. Earned Value Analysis Sample

Now, using the 50-50 rule, what would the PV and EV be for the example? The data in Figure 9.6 depict these new figures.

Since work on all three tasks has begun and none is complete, the actual and planned percents complete are all the same: 50%. This significantly changes the PV and EV values, but notice that AC is still the actual amount paid out to date. How does this affect the CV?

Task	Task Cost Estimate	Actual % Complete	Planned % Complete	PV	EV	AC
A	$1,000	50	50	$500	$500	$495
B	$1,000	50	50	$500	$500	$225
C	$800	50	50	$400	$400	$350
Total	$2,800			$1,400	$1,400	$1,070

FIGURE 9.6. Earned Value Analysis Using the 50-50 Rule

$$CV = EV - AC$$
$$= \$1,400 - \$1,070$$
$$= \$330$$

Recall that when CV was calculated earlier using different percent complete estimates, the result was CV = –$50.

The SV using the 50-50 rule becomes:

$$SV = EV - PV$$
$$= \$1,400 - \$1,400$$
$$= \$0$$

In the earlier calculation, the SV was $110, so using the 50-50 rule has its advantages. Using it on small projects with few tasks, however, can result in inaccurate analyses. In the first analysis using estimated percents complete, it was determined that the project was over budget but quite a bit ahead of schedule. With the 50-50 rule, the analysis shows that the project is under budget, by a significant amount, and is on schedule.

But don't let this apparent disadvantage dissuade you from using the technique. Just be sure to apply it when several tasks are involved and all the tasks are relatively the same in length.

Also be aware that although the 50-50 rule is the most commonly used technique of this type, other weighting techniques are also used, such as 0-100, where no credit for percent complete is given until a task is finished; 80-20, where 80% completion is assigned at the beginning of a task (particularly applicable to tasks with heavy front-end costs); 20-80; and so on. The point is that you can develop the best percent complete estimating technique for your individual project. Whatever estimating method is used, the key is to make sure it is documented and distributed to all the stakeholders so that everyone can evaluate the earned value analysis from a common perspective.

ANALYZING VARIANCE

Earned value analysis is an excellent monitoring and control technique with excellent tools to measure variances from the baseline. Variance by itself, however, is not useful until the reason for and impact of a variance can be identified and understood.

There are numerous reasons why there is variance in a project. The following are several of the most common:

■ **Estimating errors**—Inaccurately estimating the schedule or cost is probably the biggest reason for project variances. Because the baseline is built around estimates, care in estimating, constantly improving estimating techniques with lessons learned data, and updating costing models and databases will greatly reduce the variance size.

■ **Technical problems**—Technical solutions often have to be revised or changed as more is learned about the project requirements and available technology and as the design itself evolves. Sometimes technical problems do not surface until parts testing begins, which can cause significant rework of a product.

■ **Management problems**—The skill level and availability of personnel have a significant effect on whether a project can be kept on track. Too few people or people with less experience and skill than planned for a project will create a divergence from the plan. Even organizational changes (particularly in stakeholders), procedural and policy changes, and process changes or deficiencies will greatly impact whether a project stays on track.

■ **Economics and market fluctuations**—Changes in cost and changes in the market demand for a product can create a need to redefine the project scope and baseline, which causes significant variances from the original plan.

■ **Acts of nature**—Unknown or unexpected events can completely throw a project off track, even to the point of stopping a project altogether. Events such as tornadoes, fires, and floods cause large variance spikes.

■ **Subcontractors and vendors**—Without a subcontract management system that keeps subcontractors and vendors on track, the project schedule and cost variances will suffer. When a subcontract is put in place, it is important to ensure there is a requirement for status reports that support the contracting organization's own status reporting system and data format. This is the only way to get schedule and cost information in a timely way and in a format that is compatible.

- **Lead times**—Component and material lead times have to be planned for early in a project. For most projects, lead times are not a problem, but everyone sooner or later will encounter a project that has some unique material requirement or some technology or component that requires extra time to find, design, build, or ship. Planning well ahead so that lead times do not impact the schedule can make a project run a lot more smoothly.

The final step in the variance analysis process is to document the results and distribute them to the appropriate stakeholders.

STATUS REPORTING

Ultimately, communication in the project environment will determine the extent of project success. If there is no communications plan in place or if communication is loosely defined, then the chance of success is greatly reduced.

Reporting status can be achieved in a lot of different ways. Most of us use e-mail, the telephone, formal and informal reports or memoranda, formal and informal meetings, and myriad other ways to communicate. The method(s) is not as important as ensuring that everyone understands when and how status will be transmitted.

The communications plan is a part of the overall project plan. It specifies who is to receive reports, how much and how frequently information is to be disseminated, and how this information is to be transmitted. The communications plan is formally documented and is distributed to all stakeholders so that there is no doubt as to what information they will receive and when they will receive it.

One excellent tool for collecting the project data in a usable and understandable fashion is the *earned value report*. Figure 9.7 is a sample of this report. It contains all the information discussed in this section of the book that is key to earned value analysis. Most project management software packages include such a report as a part of the report generation module. Although the layout might vary slightly, generally all such reports contain the same information.

One of the key things to remember about the earned value report is that not all stakeholders know how to interpret the information. Therefore, it is

Reporting Period: _____ to _____

Project Name:	Project Control No.:	Preparer Name:	Preparer Signature:
Customer:	Customer Contact:	Contact Phone:	Date Prepared:

WBS Item No./Description	Current Period					Cumulative to Date					Estimate at Completion		
	Budgeted Cost		Actual Cost of Work	Variance		Budgeted Cost		Actual Cost of Work	Variance		Project Budget	Latest Revised Estimate	Variance
	Planned Value	Earned Value		Cost	Schedule	Planned Value	Earned Value		Cost	Schedule			

FIGURE 9.7. Sample Earned Value Report Form (Page 1)

Explanation of Variances:

Risks or Issues That Caused Variances:

Strategies to Correct Variances:

Expected Issues for the Next Reporting Period:

FIGURE 9.7.   Sample Earned Value Report Form (Page 2)

wise to hand-deliver the report and explain what the data show, at least the first time a report is issued. Another way of ensuring that everyone understands the earned value analysis is to present and explain the data in a formal meeting.

SUMMARY

Earned value management is the accepted and preferred technique for monitoring and controlling a project. It has been used by the U.S. government and by government contractors for approximately 20 years. During the late 1980s and early 1990s, the technique gained acceptance in the private sector and is now used in every industry throughout the world. It is the method of choice of the Project Management Institute for project monitoring and control.

The primary advantage of earned value management is that not only can the actual costs of a project be measured and tracked against the projected cost plan, but scheduled progress can also be measured in a way that clearly shows budget and schedule progress. Furthermore, earned value analyses provide accurate forecasting, so that schedule and budget can be adjusted to maintain the planned projections.

10

UNDERSTANDING THE PROJECT CHANGE PROCESS

Change in projects is inevitable for many reasons. Technology changes rapidly, often before an organization can get its product to market. In addition, businesses, business processes, and business models constantly have to adapt to the economic climate, competitive pressures, and the opportunity to create through change and innovation. Even without these change-altering events, the potential for change is always present in a project simply because of the number of people involved. Anyone can suggest a change! Every stakeholder and every person working on any part of any task can influence or even directly change the project scope—in spite of the fact that scope change should never be done except by the customer. Therefore, it is crucial that a formal change process be in place.

At first glance, one might assume that all organizations have a formal change process in place, but many organizations do not. Instead, when change does occur, it is either not handled, which leads to scope creep, or it is handled as a "workaround," which means that it is dealt with when it happens but with no prior planning or procedures to incorporate the change smoothly. In these organizations, there also is great misunderstanding about change definitions, documentation requirements, communication requirements, and, of course, what is entailed in developing a change control system.

This chapter discusses change management, the change management process, change control, and configuration management, as well as the key change process components and process stakeholders.

WHAT IS A PROJECT CHANGE PROCESS?

There are, in fact, two change processes or procedures in place for every project—or there should be if change management and change control are to be successful. The first change process is defined by the customer. It is a part of the contract and deals with the process of how the scope is to be changed by the customer. The second is an internal organizational process that deals with recommended changes to a product as the design and development mature. This is the process that enables the providing organization to make recommended changes to the customer.

Within an organization, change management generally occurs at two levels. At one level, the project manager recommends modifications directly to the customer if they do not affect the budget or schedule above some predetermined level, which is set by senior management. Most often, this level is either a monetary level that is not to exceed a predetermined amount of money or a time-impact level that does not slow the project down more than some predetermined amount of time. In such cases, the project manager usually makes the decision whether or not to accept a suggested change. Of course, the best of cases occurs when a suggested change can be implemented with no impact at all on scope. At the second level, a change control board considers all recommended modifications that are beyond the project manager's limit of authority.

The key to a successful project change process is for the process to be in place, documented, and communicated to the customer, all stakeholders, and all team members when a project begins so that there is no misunderstanding about the process when a change occurs. The project manager—more than anyone else—must have a thorough understanding of the process in order to eliminate scope creep and to aid in general project control. It is important, however, that the change management process is viewed in the proper perspective and that all stakeholders understand how change management fits into the project control and management structure.

In fact, there is considerable confusion and overlap among the three major terms that describe the project change environment: configuration management, change management, and change control. These terms are often used—erroneously—synonymously. Therefore, it is important to understand what these terms mean and how they relate within the total change management environment.

CONFIGURATION MANAGEMENT

In the early 1990s, "configuration" generally referred to the various changes to a basic product that could be chosen by a customer. For example, a computer company could build a basic or standard computer model with specific speed, operating characteristics, and installed tools. However, a customer could purchase a deluxe configuration with higher speed, greater memory capability, expanded operating characteristics, and so on. This second version was referred to as a configuration change. Configuration management, then, was the management of these various configuration changes.

Configuration management has come to mean much more since the days of controlling different versions of computer models. Today, the term configuration management has several different meanings. The most comprehensive or encompassing meaning is:

> The management of features and assurances through control of changes made to hardware, software, firmware, documentation, test, test fixtures, and test documentation of a system throughout the development and operational life of the system.

There are different types of configuration management—hardware, software, and operational—and it is easy to see why change management and configuration management are confused and used synonymously, but they are different. In a very real sense, configuration management is a subset of the overall change management process. Change management deals more with the process of managing changes to a project, which include the administrative processes of evaluating recommended changes from various sources, including those of the customer. Configuration management, then, deals with the change process associated with approved changes to the actual product.

CRITICAL STEPS IN CREATING A CHANGE MANAGEMENT PROCESS

Change management can be divided into two basic areas:

- Plan for change
- Manage change

Plan for Change

Change planning is a process that identifies the risk level of a change and builds requirements for change planning in order to ensure that a change is successful. The key steps in change planning for an information technology project are:

- Assign all potential changes a risk level before a change is scheduled.
- Document at least three risk levels with corresponding requirements for change planning. Identify risk levels for software and hardware upgrades, topology changes, routing changes, configuration changes, and new deployments. Assign higher risk levels to nonstandard add, move, or change types of activity.
- The high-risk change process that is identified may require lab validation, vendor review, peer review, and detailed configuration and design documentation.
- Create solution templates for deployments that affect multiple sites. Include information about physical layout, logic design, configuration, software versions, acceptable hardware chassis and modules, and deployment guidelines.
- For information technology projects, document network standards for configuration, software version, hardware supported, domain name system (DNS), device naming, design, and services supported.

Manage Change

Change management is the process to approve and schedule a change in order to ensure the correct level of notification, minimal user impact, and customer buy-in and approval. The key steps in change management for typical IT applications are:

- Assign a change controller, to assist the project manager. The change controller can run change management review meetings, receive and review change requests, manage change process improvements, and act as a liaison for user groups.
- Hold periodic change review meetings with all parties impacted.
- Document change input requirements, including change owner, business impact, risk level, reason for change, success factors, back-out or withdrawal plan, and testing requirements.
- Document change output requirements, including updates to DNS, network map, template, IP addressing, circuit management, network management, and all hardware components and services.
- Define a change approval process that verifies validation steps for higher risk change.
- Hold postmortem meetings to examine unsuccessful changes in order to determine the root cause of change failure.

The different steps in completing a change management process are shown in Figure 10.1.

A proposed change should include a complete technical definition and the intent or purpose of the change. In addition, the person or department requesting the change should include information that describes who is affected, both during the change period and after deployment. This might include business units, user groups, servers, and applications.

In general, IT project changes usually can be categorized as one or more of the following:

- Implementation of enhanced features
- Enhanced or reduced product functionality
- Design and feature enhancements
- Support for additional protocols or options

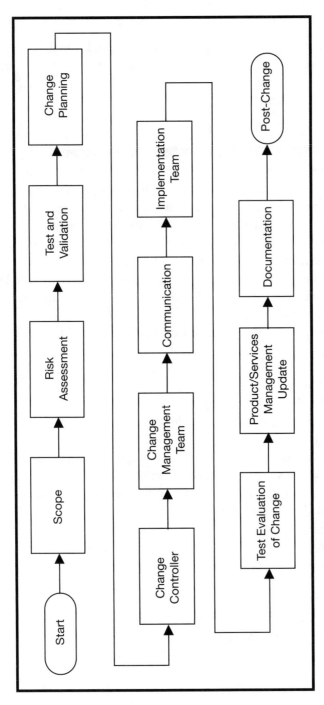

FIGURE 10.1.   High-Level Flow Diagram of a Planned Change Management Process

- Network expansion
- Addition of network segments at existing site(s)
- Addition of new sites
- Connection to existing networks or new or different hardware/software interfaces
- Software release upgrades
- Distributed client software
- Configuration changes
- Corporate mergers or acquisitions

Scope

The scope of a requested change is necessary because it defines the baseline as well as the recommended change so that the reviewer can determine if the recommended change has merit. Hence, a very precise description of the function, design, or other characteristic of the product or service to be changed is needed to form the baseline.

There are actually two parts to the scope, because once the description of the original product/service is written, then a second description, including the recommended change along with its added value to the original design, is provided for comparison. The focus of the scope is on the changed product or service because the rest of the change management process focuses on how these changes will be implemented in the product or service.

Risk Assessment

Every change has an associated potential risk. The party requesting a change should assess its risk level and identify its impact to the product and/or the project. One of the following risk categories, at a minimum, should be assigned to each change request:

- **High risk**—These changes have the highest impact on a product or a project. It is time consuming or difficult to back out of a high-risk change. Management must be made aware of a high-risk change and its implications, and all stakeholders must be notified.
- **Moderate risk**—These changes can critically impact a product and/or a project, although it is reasonably possible to back out of

a moderate-risk change. All stakeholders should be notified of a moderate-risk change.

■ **Low risk**—These changes have minor impact on a product and/or a project in general. Usually, the project manager has the authority to make these changes. Because it is easy to back out of low-risk changes, they rarely require more than minimal documentation.

Test and Validation

Once the risk level of a potential change is determined, the appropriate amount of testing and validation can be done. Often, a change does not require testing or validation of its efficacy, but it is always prudent to plan for testing and validation, especially if a risk might significantly impact the progress of a product or project. Of course, major changes must be tested and validated prior to incorporation into a product.

Change Planning

Change planning includes the identification of requirements, budget review, ordering the required hardware and software, identification of human resources, creation of change documentation, and the review of technical aspects of the change and change process. The project manager must create change-planning documentation such as maps, detailed implementation procedures, testing procedures, and back-out procedures. The level of planning is usually directly proportional to the risk level of a change.

To make a successful change, the project team should have the following goals for change planning:

■ Ensure all resources are identified and in place for the change.
■ Ensure a clear goal has been set and met for the change.
■ Ensure the change conforms to all organizational standards for design, configuration, version, naming conventions, and management.
■ Create a back-out procedure.
■ Define escalation paths.
■ Define affected users and downtimes for notification purposes.

Change planning includes the generation of a change request, which should be sent to the change controller. The following information should be included in the change request form:

- Project name
- Name of person requesting the change
- Date submitted
- Customer information
- Proposed change
  - Baseline description
  - Change description
  - Rationale
- Other work breakdown structure activities related to or impacted by the change
- Risk level of the change
- Approval requirements
- Impact review
- Result of the review
  - Change control board action
  - Customer decision
- Change procedures

Figure 10.2 is an example of a change request form.

In addition, a change request should reference any standards within the organization that apply to the change. This helps to ensure that the change conforms to current architecture or engineering design guidelines or constraints. Typical standards can include:

- Design guidelines
- Hardware and software supported
- Device and interface naming conventions
- Global standard configuration files
- Labeling conventions
- Interface description conventions
- Standard software versions
- Network management update requirements
- Out-of-band management requirements
- Security requirements

Change Controller

A key element in the change process is the change controller, usually an individual within an organization who acts as a coordinator for all change

CHANGE REQUEST FORM		
Document Preparation Information		
Project Name:	Date Prepared:	Document File No.:
Prepared by:	Signature:	
Project Background Information		
Project Manager:	Change Request No.:	Date Requested:
Requester:	Requester Signature:	Dept./Title:
Phone:	E-mail:	Office No.:
Customer Information		
Customer:	Contract Title and No.:	Contact Phone:
Proposed Change		
Baseline Description:		
Change Description:		
Rationale:		
Risks/Impact to Product/Project:		
Other Work Breakdown Structure Activities Impacted		
WBS No.:	Work Package Title/How Impacted:	
WBS No.:	Work Package Title/How Impacted:	
WBS No.:	Work Package Title/How Impacted:	
WBS No.:	Work Package Title/How Impacted:	
Approvals		
Name (Printed):	Signature:	Date:
Name (Printed):	Signature:	Date:
Name (Printed):	Signature:	Date:
Product/Project Impact Review		
Meeting Date/List of Attendees:		
Technical/Architectural Impact:		
Cost Impact:		
Schedule Impact:		
Performance/Quality Impact:		
Contract Impact:		
Change Control Board Action: ☐ **Approved** ☐ **Denied**		
_____ Signature, Change Control Board Chair		_____ Date
Customer Action: ☐ **Approved** ☐ **Denied**		
_____ Signature, Customer		_____ Date

FIGURE 10.2.   Sample Change Request Form

process details. The change controller often is—and should be—the project manager, but given the demands on the project manager's time, he or she often must rely on a trusted assistant to act as the change controller.

Normal job functions of the change controller include:

- Accept and review all change requests for completeness and accuracy.
- Run periodic (weekly or biweekly) change review meetings with change review board personnel.
- Present complete change requests to the change review board for business impact, priority, and change readiness review.
- Maintain a change schedule or calendar in order to prevent potential conflict.
- Publish change control meeting notes and help communicate changes to appropriate technology and user groups.
- Ensure that only authorized changes are implemented, that changes are implemented in an acceptable time frame in accordance with business requirements, that changes are successful, and that no new incidents are created as a result of a change.

In addition, the change controller should provide metrics for the purpose of improving the change management process. Examples of typical metrics to be collected are:

- Volume of changes processed per period, category, and risk level
- Average turnaround time of a change per period, category, and risk level
- Number of changes amended or rejected per period and category
- Number of change back-outs by category
- Number of changes that generate new problem incidents
- Number of changes that do not produce desired business results
- Number of emergency changes implemented
- Degree of client satisfaction

Change Management Team

The change management team includes representation from all affected groups or individuals within an organization. The team reviews all change requests and makes recommendations to the project manager, who approves or denies each request based on completeness, readiness, business impact, business need, and any conflicts. If a request exceeds the project manager's authority, it is forwarded to the change control board.

The team should first review each change in order to ensure all associated documentation is complete, based on the risk level. Then the team can investigate the business impact issues and business requirements. The final step is to schedule the change. Once a change has been approved, the change management team is also responsible for communication of the change to all parties affected. In some cases, user training might also be needed.

Communication

Once a change is approved, the next step is to communicate details of the change by setting expectations, aligning support resources, communicating operational requirements, and informing users. The risk level and potential impact to groups affected, as well as scheduled downtime as a result of the change, should dictate the communication requirements.

One excellent way to determine who is affected by a change and what the potential downtime might be for each application incorporating the change, user group, or developer group is to create a matrix showing who is affected by the change. Keep in mind that different groups might require various levels of detail about a change. For instance, support groups might receive communication with more detailed aspects of a change, new support requirements, and individual contacts, whereas user groups might simply receive a notice of the potential downtime and a short message that describes the business benefit, but developer groups may receive notice that some design in hardware and software may be required.

Implementation Team

The implementation team consists of individuals with the technical expertise to expedite a change. The implementation team should also be involved in the planning phase to contribute to the development of the project checkpoints, testing, back-out criteria, and back-out time constraints. This team should guarantee adherence to organizational standards, design standards, and organizational and project management tools and maintain and enhance the tool set used to test and validate a change.

Specifically, the implementation team should fully understand the following testing questions and should include them in the change documentation prior to approval by the change control board:

- How thoroughly should the change be tested?
- How will the test be rolled out?
- How long does testing last, and at what point can it be determined that the change has been implemented successfully?

The implementation team also should be fully aware of all back-out criteria, time constraints, and procedures. The team should answer the following questions as part of the change documentation for a high-risk change prior to approval by the change control board:

- How is the change to be removed?
- At what point is the decision made to back out the change?
- What information should be gathered before back-out occurs to determine why the change needed to be backed out or why it affected the project adversely?

During the implementation of any change, it is key to follow the change management team recommendations on how to make the change. If anything is performed on the project that deviates from the recommendations, the implementation team should document and present these steps to the change controller upon completion of the change.

Test Evaluation of Change

Testing and verification can be critical to a successful change. Testing steps to be followed should be identified, so that as a change is implemented, it can be tested at predetermined checkpoints to determine its viability with the product design. In addition, sufficient time should be allocated for testing, both during and after the implementation and back-out, if necessary. In some cases, testing can be done prior to a change when new service is involved, such as a new product function that is not currently in production.

For an IT project, some additional testing and verification procedures might be pertinent to a network change, such as:

- Extended pings for connectivity and performance
- End-user-station network and application testing
- File transfers or traffic generation for performance-related changes
- Bit error rate tester (BERT) testing for new circuits
- Interface statistic verification
- Log file verification
- Debug verification
- Display or show command verification
- Network management station availability and verification

After reaching some level of comfort with a change, it is time to evaluate what has been accomplished. Does the change make sense? Did the change address the problem? What should be done differently the next time a change is warranted?

Management Update

Operational readiness of a product requires an update to all project software and hardware management tools, device configuration, and management information systems in order to reflect a change. In addition, an organization might have tools for fault management, configuration management, availability measurement, inventory management, billing, security, and even project management processes that require updates.

Documentation

Possibly the most important requirement in any product or service environment is to have current and accurate information about the products or services available at all times. During the process of changing a product, it is critical to ensure that documentation is kept up to date. Product documentation should include the following:

- Detailed physical layer drawing that displays all devices that have a medium risk or higher on the network, including rack layouts, cable connections, and devices
- Out-of-band management access maps and documentation
- Solution templates

- Naming standards for all product devices
- Software code and hardware types currently implemented and supported
- Protocol that filters criteria and methodologies
- Routing protocol standards and supported modifications from default settings
- Global configuration standards
- Inventory database for all physical connectivity and contact information

In addition, for an information technology project, it is recommended that a matrix be developed that contains information about user groups, the applications they require, and the servers (addresses and locations) that host these applications. This information is necessary in order to ensure that users continue to have the level of access and performance they require during and after a change. In addition, previously used test plans assist in simplifying future changes, and they may assist in troubleshooting problems that occur as a result of a change.

UNDERSTANDING PROJECT CHANGE CONTROL AND CHANGE CONTROL MANAGEMENT

Control, in its basic form, entails implementing strategies to maintain the project baseline. However, projects—especially complex projects—are not simple to control. Luckily, there are steps that can be taken that make controlling a project at least manageable. Figure 10.3 shows the steps and techniques of a control process, which is applicable to any project—whether simple or complex—and can be used in any industry.

Basis of Control and Management

After a proposed change is identified, control of the project baseline is not possible without timely and accurate data from the two top boxes in Figure 10.3. The project plan is developed using cost and schedule estimates based on the technical requirements of a project. Because the baseline is only as good as the estimates, constant replanning is necessary. Actual costs are needed to measure

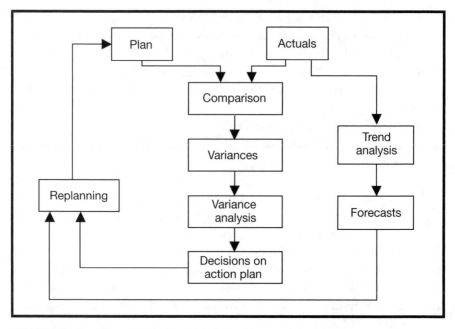

FIGURE 10.3.   Steps in Project Change Management Process

how a project is performing against the budget, and task leaders must provide accurate assessments of their progress against the schedule.

Plans and Actuals

Real-time information about the costs and schedule is imperative in order to determine how well a project is performing against the plan. One dilemma facing project managers is not having access to a management information system that can deliver actual expenditures and schedule changes in a timely manner, which is why many project managers do their own tracking. Actually, it is a good idea to maintain a tracking system within a project just to have a backup in the event the accounting system cannot deliver the cost reports when needed.

Variances, Trends, and Forecasts

A trend analysis using the actual expenditure figures can help a project team forecast how a project is likely to progress. Comparing the actuals against the plan provides information about how a project is performing against the baseline; that is, it reveals if there are variances, and if so, what they are. Therefore, the variances, along with the trends and forecasts, are vital for planning future control strategies.

Variance Analysis

Variance analysis can be accomplished using earned value management, which was discussed in detail in the last chapter. Variance analysis is the assessment of exactly how close the actual costs and schedules are to the plan and, more importantly, why there is a variance. Depending on project performance, variance can be good or bad. If a project is over budget, that is usually bad, but if a project is ahead of schedule, being over budget at some point might not be bad at all. Thus, the analysis must examine the variance to determine the cause of it and whether the variance indicates an adjustment is needed. In short, it is not enough just to determine if a project is over budget or behind schedule; it is more important to determine why a project is not on plan.

Action Plan

Once the variance and trend analyses are complete and there is a reasonable expectation about project progress for the next reporting period, it is time to develop an action plan or make decisions about how to correct the variances. The action plan depends entirely on the circumstances at that time. That is, if the variance analysis warrants it and the trend appears to worsen, then drastic measures are in order, such as add resources, hire consultants, or renegotiate scope changes. Normally, if a project team has conscientiously tracked project progress, variances are relatively small and require only managerial tightening of the procedures and processes. However, like Murphy's law, risk events do occur, and projects do tend more toward instability than stability. As a result, constant vigilance for variance is crucial in the control process.

Replanning

The project plan must be revised constantly. The early, original plan will not be sufficient or accurate for the duration of a project because as a project progresses, more is known about the requirements, risks, technical approach, and so on. Therefore, at each assessment point in a project, the plan must be validated, and usually it must be changed.

This controlling and managing process is the normal, day-to-day process for addressing changes and variances that occur merely due to the work stresses of developing and delivering a product. What happens, then, when changes are consciously introduced? Those changes fall under the purview of the change management process.

WHY A CHANGE MANAGEMENT PROCESS IS REQUIRED

Changes, unfortunately, can come from anywhere and potentially from anyone associated with a project. Even someone writing new code can change the project scope by adding enhancements that are not called for or by stripping functions that seem unnecessary. Some of the most common sources of change are:

- Customers
- Project team members
- Government agencies
- Environmental agencies or interest groups
- Product obsolescence
- Changes in managerial or organizational objectives
- Technological changes
- Funding changes

All the changes affecting a project are generally handled by one of two processes. The first process is established in the contract by the customer and deals with actual contractual/legal changes. The second process is the internal change management process that considers recommended changes to the project scope and/or product.

A change process outlined in the original contract handles those modifications that are outside the realm of a project, that is, changes from the customer or outside influences that indicate a change to the contract. The usual method for handling these modifications is a formal notice from the customer alerting the provider to the change and asking for an impact analysis. If a modification has the effect of increasing both the budget and schedule, then the customer requests a proposal, which is evaluated, negotiated, and either accepted or not. If, however, a change requires reducing the scope of the original project, then the provider is asked for an analysis of the damages to the company. In this case, damages would include such costs as hiring additional resources, renting facilities, buying equipment, and so on, and the provider may be entitled to receive fair compensation for the damages.

It is not often that the customer will reduce the scope once a project is started. However, it does happen, and when it does, customers are sensitive to losses incurred by the provider. The real problems, however, involve project managers who, in their zeal to provide the customer with more than was expected, allow changes to the project scope without an attendant contract modification. The Project Management Institute is very clear in its warning against this practice; its position is that a customer should never be given more than was stated in the project requirements. To do so is what is known as "gold-plating," which leads to higher costs for the customer or, at a minimum, leads to scope creep, which hurts both the provider and the customer.

These kinds of modifications to a project are made in accordance with the procedures that the customer sets forth. A change management process that an organization establishes and a customer approves, or at least evaluates and accepts, handles modifications that are recommended from within the organization. However, it should be noted that the customer can also use this process and will use it, depending on the significance of impact to the project. How this overlapping of change processes works out will be clarified in the discussion of the change management process and its purpose.

THE CHANGE MANAGEMENT PROCESS

Although the change management process is very straightforward, the results can be significant and occasionally disastrous if it is not followed. The objective of the change management process is to ensure a central control point for all recommended changes to a project. The emphasis here is on "all recommended changes." The implication is that no changes are made without first going through a rigorous recommendation and evaluation process. This

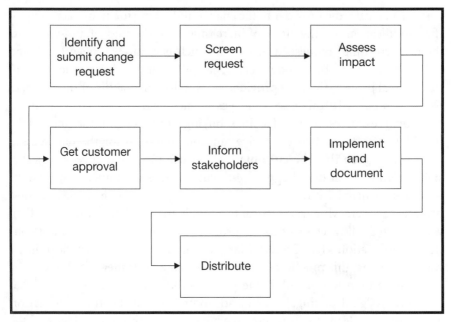

FIGURE 10.4.   Flow Diagram of a Product Change

process is designed to eliminate scope creep and gold-plating and to maintain the integrity of the project plan. A flow diagram of the change management process is depicted in Figure 10.4. A detailed discussion of each step in the process follows.

As stated earlier, anyone can recommend changes. Often, as a project matures, it becomes obvious that certain functions do not work well or that additional or different functions might work better. When this occurs, a change recommendation should be documented with some very specific information, such as who is making the recommendation, what the recommended change is, when it should be done (i.e., at what stage of the product development), what its value will be, and what the estimated impact is on the project.

In some organizations, the project manager can assess a recommended change and make a decision to go to the customer for approval. Normally, this kind of authority is granted based on some level of estimated impact on the project schedule, budget, and/or scope. Above that level of authority, however, the project manager is required to make an assessment and send it to a change control board (CCB), which is an ad hoc committee of three to five members.

In all cases, a recommended change(s) should funnel through the project manager regardless of whether the request is within the project manager's authority limits or whether it must be escalated to the CCB. In fact, the project manager should be the moderator or facilitator of any CCB meetings.

Of course, all change requests must be communicated to all stakeholders. One excellent tool for documenting a change request or recommendation is the *change control form,* an example of which is shown in Figure 10.5.

Generally, the person recommending a change has a good sense of what effect the change will have on the project because he or she most likely is the person who will make the change if it is approved. This, however, is not always true; sometimes the impact of a change is not fully understood by the person who requests it. In all cases, the project manager should assess a change request and its effect on the triple constraint of cost, time, and scope for the CCB's consideration. Other considerations are equally important, such as the effect on other functional areas, stakeholder interests, organizational politics, the team and its workload, quality, and the management of the project itself.

If the CCB accepts the recommendation for a change to a project, its decision does not mean that the change is automatically put in place. Rather, it means that the CCB or its designated representative will present the recommendation to the customer for approval. The customer's acceptance of a change is formalized by a contract amendment.

Occasionally, a customer will assume the role of a stakeholder or team member just to assess the reaction of the provider to a change suggestion. This is done within the change management process rather than through the contractual process because it may not be known how much—if any—impact there will be to the project schedule, budget, or scope. The process then follows its normal course through the CCB, with the customer acting as an interested stakeholder or interested party but without the authority or status of CCB membership. The customer then decides whether or not to pursue the change, depending on the results of the impact evaluation and the CCB's recommendation. This process can significantly reduce the time required for change approval.

Up to now, what has been discussed is the process involved when a change is approved. What is the process if a change is not approved? The

CHANGE CONTROL FORM			
Project Name:	Change Control Ref. No.:	Prepared by:	Preparer Signature:
Customer:	Customer Contact:	Contact Phone:	Date:

Initiator Information

Change Requester:	Requester's Title and Organization:
Phone:	E-mail:

Change Information

Nature of change:

Is change out of scope   ☐ Yes   ☐ No
If change is out of scope, complete the following.

Detail the technical impact of the proposed change:

Detail the cost impact of the proposed change:

Detail the schedule impact of the proposed change:

Change authority signature:

Change Control Board Chairman/Project Manager   Date

FIGURE 10.5. Sample Change Control Form

process is the same through CCB consideration. If a change is not approved, however, the request and the reasons for its rejection are documented, the person who made the change request is notified with an explanation of why it was rejected, and the documentation is added to the project binder for historical purposes.

When a modification is approved and implemented, what does that mean to the project manager and the project plan? Every time a project is changed, the project plan must be updated. This primarily means there is an amendment to the work breakdown structure (WBS). Remember, if something isn't in the WBS, it is not a part of the project. Thus, if there is a change to the scope—no matter how small the change, then the WBS must reflect the change.

Once a modification becomes effective and the WBS is amended, every stakeholder must be informed. No change occurs without a complete document and communication update. Unless everyone is aware of a change, it cannot be fully implemented. Likewise, if a modification is not approved or incorporated, the person who initiated the change request must be notified and the action must be recorded. Changes, whether implemented or not, become a part of the project documentation for future reference.

When a change is recommended and approved by the customer, the plan must be updated. Often, accepted recommended modifications involve contractual amendments. In some ways, changing the contract is of great benefit to the management process because a formal amendment to a contract forces a plan revision. Regrettably, this formalization is not usually done for internal projects, and it is often left to the project manager to ensure that all of the proper documentation and plan updating are accomplished. Because the lack of a formal contractual process sometimes means that a change to a project is not adequately incorporated, project managers need to remember that it is their responsibility to ensure that a change is properly presented, accepted (or rejected), and updated in the project plan.

Updating the project plan starts with an update to the WBS. Every modification to a project should be reflected as a task in the WBS; the network analysis, schedules, budgets, and so on can thereafter be refreshed.

The next step in the change management process is to communicate the action of a recommendation to the appropriate people. Communicating a modification is just as important as making the decision to implement a change in the first place. The key roles in the communication process fall to the customer's project manager and the organizational project manager.

The customer's project manager informs the customer stakeholders and ensures that all documentation, direction, funding, and all other contractual obligations are in place. The project manager who is responsible for the project work informs all the organizational stakeholders about the change. Two additional tools are very useful for communication and change tracking: the change responsibility form and the document control form.

The *change responsibility form* is used to record a change. One form is used for each change to ensure accurate tracking. The form lists the individuals involved in a change, their responsibilities for ensuring the change is properly made, and a description of the change itself. A sample of this document is provided in Figure 10.6.

The *document control form* is used to track the communications regarding a project change. Its specific importance is to record the historical events relative to a modification. This form is important not only for the lessons learned archive, but can also be crucial in the event of litigation after a project ends. Accordingly, being able to show the sequence of events may be as important as an event itself. A sample document control form is provided in Figure 10.7.

The process of change management is not difficult, but it is important. Without both the contractual change process and the internal change request process in place, the project manager's ability to control scope creep can be quite difficult.

SUMMARY

Change requests can come from anyone, which creates the need for a formalized change management process. Change requests usually come from stakeholders, in particular team members, but sometimes they come from external sources, such as environmental groups or regulatory agencies. If a change request comes from the customer, there is a contractual process through which the change is managed. Under no circumstances should a change be implemented before a contract modification is in place.

The project manager is the focal point for all change requests. Many organizations allow the project manager some latitude relative to whether to approve a change request. Generally, the limits of project manager authority have to do with how much impact there is to the budget or to the schedule

CHANGE RESPONSIBILITY FORM			
Project Name:	Project Reference No.:	Prepared by:	Preparer Signature:
Customer:	Customer Contact:	Contact Phone:	Date Prepared:

Project Manager

Phone:	E-mail:	Office Location:

Responsibilities:

Customer Project Manager:

Phone:	E-mail:	Office Location:

Responsibilities:

Change Control Board (list members):

Responsibilities:

Other Stakeholder Interested Parties (list names):

Responsibilities:

FIGURE 10.6. Sample Change Responsibility Form

DOCUMENT CONTROL FORM			
Project Name:	Project Reference No.:	Prepared by:	Preparer Signature:
Customer:	Customer Contact:	Contact Phone:	Date Prepared:

Document Distribution

Name of Recipient	Title	Organizational Code

Change History

Date of Change Request	Change Description	Action/Authority

FIGURE 10.7. **Sample Document Control Form**

and, of course, whether there is any impact to the scope. If a change request is within scope, then usually the change is made, with a simple notification to the customer and other stakeholders.

The change control process includes numerous change control documents. Key among these are the following:

- Change request form
- Change control form
- Change responsibility form
- Document control form

It is also very important to remember that each change request has associated with it a potential risk. Therefore, every change request should be accompanied by a complete risk impact analysis.

SUCCESSFULLY CLOSING THE PROJECT

The closing phase of a project is often the most difficult phase. Project team members are either concerned about whether they have a new project to work on or are being actively moved to other projects, because functional managers are constantly under pressure to begin new projects or because a shortage of resources—also a common dilemma in most organizations—requires personnel reassignment even before a project is completely closed out. Also, when a project has been a long-term endeavor of, say, three to five years and the project environment has become "home" for the team members, people have been known to actually sabotage their work to drag it out and keep the project from ending. All these distractions occur while the project manager is busily trying to complete the deliverables and take care of the requisite administrative and contractual requirements, and often he or she is left with inadequate resources to complete the tasks.

There are many activities required in the closeout process, but the number of activities is not the measure—what has to be done and the criticality of performing the activities accurately and completely finally determine the measure of project success. The wise project manager starts planning for closeout at the beginning of a project so that there are no surprises or shortfalls when the customer accepts the project deliverables.

Basically, there are three things the project team needs to be aware of and be prepared to do in order to complete a project:

- Determine when the project is complete
- Evaluate the project plan in the context of project completion
- Provide concrete measurements of project success at project completion

This chapter discusses how each of these objectives is accomplished.

HOW TO DETERMINE PROJECT COMPLETION

Determining when a project is completed is not always easy. If asked how to determine when a project is completed, most project team members would answer that a project is finished when all the work is done. But that is not the measure of project completion; the measure of completion is when the customer accepts the deliverables that were agreed to before the project began. Therefore, the short answer to when a project is completed is when the customer is satisfied. Thus the question becomes: How does one satisfy the customer? There are two ways: evaluate the project plan to determine completion of the tasks and satisfy the customer's acceptance criteria.

EVALUATE THE PROJECT PLAN TO DETERMINE PROJECT COMPLETION

The project plan is built upon the work breakdown structure (WBS), which is the basis for the project scope. Verifying the scope requires a careful review of the WBS to ensure that all tasks have been completed. If any task is left unfinished, then the project is not complete. On the other hand, it is a mistake to assume a project is complete just because all WBS tasks have been accomplished. In the absence of acceptance criteria from the customer, regardless of whether the WBS tasks are completed, a project is not completed until the customer accepts the deliverables and responsibility for the project.

PROVIDE CONCRETE MEASUREMENTS FOR PROJECT COMPLETION

A crucial mistake made by inexperienced project managers or those managing internal projects is not requiring agreed-to and written acceptance criteria. In a formal contract with a customer outside the organization, specific acceptance criteria should be included in the contract language. If there are none, the customer can forever claim that the deliverable is not exactly what was requested and the project continues. Likewise, projects internal to an organization—especially those that involve different organizational groups—will suffer the same consequences if there is not a memorandum of agreement among the groups that specifically details the acceptance criteria.

OTHER PROJECT COMPLETION ACTIVITIES

No matter how well a project has been controlled up to this point, there are three issues that—if not handled properly—will destabilize a project and can actually result in an unsuccessful project:

- Scope verification
- Contract closeout
- Administrative closure

Scope Verification

Scope verification is formalized acceptance by the stakeholders that the team has completed what was requested by the customer and documented in the project plan. Scope verification is sometimes wrongfully thought to be checking the scope at the beginning of a project to ensure that everything in the scope statement is captured in the plan. Actually, scope verification occurs at the *end* of tasks, phases, and, most importantly, at the end of a project. This is the time to determine that everything has been completed as advertised.

Contract Closeout

Contract closeout is the administrative closure of all the contractual requirements. This includes special terms and conditions and financial audits to ensure bills have been paid and invoices issued. Also included is verification that all deliverables, reports, and documentation are complete and the customer has accepted the product or service.

Administrative Closure

Administrative closure means verifying that all reports have been written, including and especially the final project report, and all information has been disseminated to the stakeholders. Then the project is formally closed.

Reassign Resources

The preceding three issues are the key ones that *must* be accomplished, but the project manager has other activities to complete. One of the most important is to reassign resources and equipment.

Often, a project involves buying or renting equipment and facilities or even using equipment from the customer. All this equipment has to be accounted for and returned to its rightful owner.

As far as project team members are concerned, the project manager is responsible for either reassigning them, if he or she has that authority, or, at a minimum, making recommendations for their future role within the company.

EXIT STRATEGY PROCESS

The work of closing a project is not easy and it is certainly not trivial, but it can go a lot more smoothly if an exit strategy process is in place. Every project should have a formalized exit strategy because missing even one step in the process could mean failure for an otherwise successful project. Figure 11.1 depicts a process that can be used for any kind of project. The user simply needs to fill in the activity details that best meet the needs of his or her industry and organization.

The steps in this process should be designed to examine every aspect of a project, including the contract for a project done for a customer external to the organization or other documents such as the statement of work for a project done for an internal customer. The steps also should be designed to ensure all the stakeholders are involved with project closure and that their expectations have been met. To understand more fully how the process works, it is beneficial to examine each step in some detail.

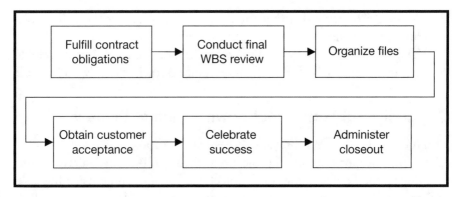

FIGURE 11.1.   The Exit Strategy Process

Fulfill Contract Obligations

If one of the steps in the exit strategy process is more important than any other, it has to be this one. One of the difficulties in completing this step is that contract terms can be verbal or written, although written ones are easier to enforce, and correspondence generated throughout the life cycle of a project can assume the force of a legal document. Therefore, a thorough internal review of the project requirements, written and verbal promises, and deliverables is crucial.

Along these lines, it is worthwhile mentioning that a detailed record of all interactions with the customer is crucial, not just for the sake of ensuring everything promised is delivered, but for the protection of both the customer and the provider. For example, if a team member attends a meeting with the customer and promises or agrees to something during the meeting, that promise—even if verbal—has behind it the weight of the project manager and the organization and can be enforced by the customer. If the team member fails to report the promise and it is not recorded, then a final review of the project deliverables may reveal a nasty surprise. In fact, it is this kind of occurrence that is the largest contributor to scope creep.

In addition to handing off the project deliverables, there are two other very important required activities. The first is a financial review to ensure the bills have been paid and, very important, that the customer receives the final invoice. The second is that the customer must accept the deliverables in writing. Otherwise, the project cannot end.

The first and second steps in the process actually overlap, but it is useful to consider them separately so that the importance of each is clearly understood.

Conduct Final Work Breakdown Structure Review

Conducting the final WBS review serves many purposes. The WBS is, after all, the most important tool in project management. It is particularly important during the final activities of a project because it documents all the tasks and the individual work packages required to design, develop, and deliver the product. Therefore, the final review is designed to determine whether every single work package is complete, and if any is not, why not and whether it now needs to be completed.

The project scope can change during the life cycle of a project, and the WBS should reflect these changes. Remember that if something is not in the WBS, then it is not in the project. The final review will reveal whether the WBS was changed to reflect differences between the original scope and the final scope. This technical audit, incidentally, also can be used to check the financial audit. That is, revisiting each work package allows the project team to determine if the bills have been paid and every legitimate charge has been invoiced.

Organize Files

Organizing the files includes three subparts, and each is important to the success of future projects. It is a good idea to keep an index or content list of all files for future use. Data in project files vary from formal, such as status or progress reports, to informal, such as the project manager's notes from a team meeting. Generally, all the records are important because they provide a trail that supports any actions taken to achieve the project results. Furthermore, they may substantiate whether verbal agreements were made during meetings with the customer or other stakeholders.

Project data usually fall into one of three broad categories:

- **Working or day-by-day documents**—All documents needed to run a project. These include such documents as the Gantt charts (i.e., schedules), analyses, status reports, progress reports, change management, and so on. Keeping these data together facilitates any technical reviews or audits.

- **Contract or legal documents**—All documents that relate to an external contract or to the statement of work, charter, or memoranda with the customer.
- **Lessons learned**—Analyses of what went right and what went wrong during a project. These analyses are particularly important for future projects because they not only can improve the estimating process but also can mitigate risks.

Measures are established in the project-planning process in part so that metrics can be collected and analyzed for the following reasons:

- To gain a better understanding of processes, products, resources, and environments and to establish baselines for comparisons with future assessments.
- To determine project status with respect to plans. Measures are indicators of when projects and processes are drifting off track, so they can be brought back under control. Analysis also assesses achievement of quality goals and the impact of technology and process improvements on products and processes.
- To gain an understanding of relationships among processes and products, so the values observed can be used to predict others. This is done to establish achievable goals for cost, schedule, quality, and performance, so that appropriate resources can be applied. This analysis also is the basis for trending, so that estimates for cost and schedule—as well as quality—can be updated based upon current and more accurate evidence than was available during project planning.
- Perhaps the most important reason to establish measures and collect and analyze metrics is to identify roadblocks, root causes, inefficiencies, and other opportunities for improving product quality and process performance. Current performance gives us baselines to compare whether or not improvement actions are working as intended and what the side effects may be. Good measures also help communicate goals and convey reasons for improving—an excellent opportunity to engage and focus the support of those working within processes to make them successful.

The main objective of having an integrated measurement and metrics analysis methodology is to objectively measure the program health and status in relation to improving the following goals of an organization:

- **Project management**—Planning, estimating, monitoring, and controlling a project's costs, schedules, and quality
- **Process improvement**—Providing baseline data and measuring trends, tracking root causes of problems and defects, and identifying and implementing changes for process improvement
- **Organizational vision**—Effectively applying unified end-to-end engineering processes and methods that encompass proven and emerging standards or approaches for the purpose of delivering high-quality, cost-competitive system solutions to customers.

Most companies do a reasonably good job with the first two types of documentation, but almost none do a good job with the lessons learned. The problem is that by the time a lessons learned session is scheduled, most of the team members have been reassigned to other projects. Still, the importance of collecting the lessons learned experience cannot be overemphasized.

Finalizing Customer Relationships

Organizing the files is very important, but equally important is finalizing customer relationships. Actually, "finalizing" is the wrong word here—the relationship should be such that it is ongoing so that customers remain happy and will issue contracts for future business. After all, one of the key corporate objectives of any project is that it makes customers so happy they want to come back with other projects.

Finalizing customer relationships in the context of an exit strategy means that now is the time to ensure the customer is completely happy with and eager to accept the project deliverables. It is also the time to talk about bridging the gap between product acceptance and signing up for some ongoing maintenance, if that is appropriate for the project. At the very least, it is the time to establish a relationship that allows periodic discussions about how the deliverables are serving the customer's needs and whether there might be additional work for the provider organization in the near future.

Often, a project does have an option for continuing maintenance and servicing. Usually, in these instances, a different corporate group is responsible for this function. In that case, this step is the appropriate place to make sure the project is handed off properly and the customer is aware of who the key contact and players are. Not only is it good project management procedure, but it is also good business.

Celebrate Success

It is a mistake not to celebrate the success of a project. Many organizations miss out on the opportunity to properly close out a project as a team and to acknowledge everyone's hard work. Celebrating a project's close and success serves three purposes. First, it marks the official end of the project for the project team. Second, it does provide the opportunity to acknowledge everyone and their individual contributions to the success of the project. Finally, as a leader, the project manager can only gain from this show of appreciation. This will be apparent the next time that project manager heads up a project and needs a new team.

The lessons learned review often takes place during this celebratory time, and it is a good time to collect additional lessons learned data. However, the essence of the lessons learned effort should be complete before this time because team members are already thinking about their new assignments. Still, the astute project manager will take the opportunity of the celebration to record the members' recollections of what went right and what went wrong.

Administer Closeout

The final step in the exit strategy process is to actually formally close out the project. There are three things left to do to close out a project at this stage of its life cycle. The first is to reassign the personnel who have worked on the project. The second is to redistribute any materials or equipment used in designing, developing, and producing the project, especially if provided by the customer or another group in the organization. The third is to circulate and archive all the project documentation.

Reassigning personnel is not always an option for the project manager. Most often, the team members and all those who have supported the project work actually report to a functional manager and not directly to the project manager. Therefore, the project manager may not have the responsibility or authority to reassign personnel. If that is the case, the project manager should produce written recommendations for each team member so that their functional managers, and they, know how they performed on the task work. This serves two purposes. First, feedback, especially constructive feedback, is helpful to the person and to his or her manager for purposes of career advancement. But just as important, this evaluation serves to identify those who would do good work on future projects. It is beneficial to the organization as a whole, and it is in the project manager's unique purview to perform this function.

Redistributing materials and equipment can be an arduous and time-consuming task. Many projects use government- or customer-furnished equipment to aid in developing the project product. All this equipment must be accounted for and returned to the proper owner. Furthermore, many projects require facilities that have to be rented and provisioned. It is the project manager's job to ensure all the facilities and any equipment are distributed or closed out properly.

The final act in this process is to circulate the appropriate documentation, particularly the final project report, and to archive the project documentation. The project binder(s) that contains the technical documentation, the contractual documentation, and the lessons learned has to be placed where it can be retrieved easily for future reference.

SUMMARY

The closeout phase of a project is often the most difficult because team members are already looking for new assignments or, worse, functional managers are pulling their personnel off the project for reassignment to new start-up projects. Additional difficulties arise simply because the closeout process is not simple and requires attention to a lot of legal, financial, and technical detail.

Some key points to remember during this process are:

- Closeout is a process—not an event.
- Project managers must ensure that all steps are taken to close out a project properly.
- Many stakeholders are involved in project closeout.
- Conducting lessons learned reviews is critical to future project and organizational success.

Finally, remember that the metrics collected from a project should be analyzed, documented, and integrated into the company's databases, so that estimating and planning techniques can be continually improved.

APPENDIX:
TOOLS AND
TEMPLATES

TOOLS FOR CHAPTER 1: INTRODUCTION

Tool 1.1 is not so much a tool as it is a guide to what can be expected in the life cycle of a project. The graphic depicts a typical project life cycle, with the associated activities the project manager and his or her team might expect to encounter. The value of this type of graphic is that it helps clarify what the typical activities are during each phase of a project and, therefore, suggests to the project manager what tools can best be used to address the activities.

Tool 1.2 is a binder content outline for a project. One of the very first things a project manager does is set up a project binder; actually, it usually ends up being several binders. The project binder is nothing more than a collection of binders that contain the various important documents associated with a project—for example, contract documents, status reports, change management documents, and so on. Tool 1.2 is a guide to the various components in the project binder.

Tool 1.3 is a project charter outline, which authorizes a project and designates the project manager who is in charge. The charter is the output of the concept phase of a project.

Tool 1.4 is the project requirements document (PRD). The PRD would logically fall in the next chapter on requirements, but because project phases cannot be neatly defined, and since requirements are the heart of any project, it is not unusual for the PRD to be started early in a project. This is particularly true because project failure is most often attributed to misinterpretation of or poorly written requirements. Therefore, preparation of the PRD should begin as early as possible. Other tools to aid in this process can be found in the tools for Chapter 2.

Concept	Planning	Design and Development	Implementation	Closeout

■ Gather data
■ Identify need
■ Establish:
  □ Goals, objectives
  □ Basic economics, feasibility
  □ Stakeholders
  □ Risk level
  □ Strategy
  □ Potential team
■ Guesstimate resources
■ Identify alternatives
■ Present proposal
■ Obtain approval for next phase
	■ Appoint key team members
	■ Conduct studies
	■ Develop scope baseline:
	  □ End product(s)
	  □ Quality standards
	  □ Resources
	  □ Activities
	■ Establish:
	  □ Master plan
	  □ Budget, cash flow
	  □ Work breakdown structure
	  □ Policies and procedures
	■ Assess risks
	■ Confirm justification
	■ Present project brief
	■ Obtain approval to proceed
		■ Set up:
		  □ Organization
		  □ Communications
		■ Motivate team
		■ Detail technical requirements
		■ Establish:
		  □ Work packages
		  □ Information control systems
		■ Procure goods and services
		■ Execute work packages
			■ Direct/monitor/ forecast/control:
			  □ Scope
			  □ Quality
			  □ Time
			  □ Cost
			■ Resolve problems
				■ Finalize product(s)
				■ Review and accept
				■ Settle final accounts
				■ Transfer product responsibility
				■ Evaluate project
				■ Document results
				■ Release/redirect resources
				■ Reassign project team

TOOL 1.1. Typical Activities During a Project Life Cycle

Project Name:	Project Control No.:	Prepared by:	Preparer Signature:
Customer:	Customer Contact:	Contact Phone:	Date Prepared:

Contents	File Location	Update Information
Project Plan (include work breakdown structure, schedules, budgets, and index to ancillary plans):		
Contract Requirements (include copy of contract, statement of work, subcontracts):		
Audit Reports:		
Status Reports:		
Correspondence:		

TOOL 1.2. Project Binder Content Outline

Contents	File Location	Update Information
Change Control Actions:		
Meetings:		
Tests and Acceptance:		
Supporting Plans:		
Lessons Learned Document:		

TOOL 1.2.   Project Binder Content Outline (continued)

PROJECT CHARTER

Project Name:	Project Ref./ID No.:	Preparer Name:	Preparer Signature:
Customer:	Customer Contact:	Contact Phone:	Date Prepared:

To (distribution):

From (initiating authority):

Assignment (include project manager's name, name of the project, customer's name):

Project Manager's Responsibility (describe the extent of the project manager's responsibility relative to planning, implementing, and delivering the project's product[s] or service[s]):

Project Manager's Authority (describe the level of project manager authority and the mechanisms and trigger points for escalating project issues to higher authority):

Functional Support (list all functional organizations and describe their responsibilities to the project):

Project Scope (briefly describe the scope and how the project supports the organization's strategic plan):

Authorizing Signature	**Title**	**Date**

TOOL 1.3.   Project Charter

PROJECT REQUIREMENTS DOCUMENT

Project Name:	Project Ref. No.:	Preparer Name:	Preparer Signature:
Customer:	Customer Contact:	Contact Phone:	Date Prepared:

Project Summary/Background

Project Objectives/Deliverables

Key Milestones

Assumptions and Constraints

Risks

Key Resource Requirements

Acceptance Criteria

Interrelated Projects

Reviews

Communications Plan

Change Management Plan

Financial Analysis

Signatures

TOOL 1.4. Project Requirements Document

TOOLS FOR CHAPTER 2: IDENTIFYING AND DEVELOPING CUSTOMER REQUIREMENTS

Tool 2.1 is the requirements record. This is a simple form that is used to identify each individual record. One of the problems in determining all the requirements for a project is that too many teams do not take the time to identify each requirement separately. This form is an aid in doing exactly that. Tool 2.1a is a sample completed requirements record.

Tool 2.2 is the statement of work format. A statement of work describes a project and what the project deliverables are.

Tool 2.3 is a checklist for making a bid/no-bid decision. One of the big problems in organizations today is ending projects once they start. The reality is that an organization must be willing to end a project that is not contributing to its strategic goals or strategic business plan. This tool provides a checklist of questions or issues that should be addressed when such decisions are considered.

Tool 2.4 is the stakeholder assessment worksheet. It is vitally important to identify all the stakeholders for a project. Many projects fail because the project manager does not identify and engage the stakeholders in the project business. This tool helps to identify and assess the stakeholders, so that the project manager knows who the stakeholders are and also what their influence is on the project. One critical aspect of stakeholder analysis that many project managers miss is developing strategies for winning stakeholders that are neutral or negative so that they become project champions. This tool helps clarify what has to be done to achieve this positive goal.

REQUIREMENTS RECORD

Project Title:

Project Manager: Date:

Customer:

Customer Contact: Contact Phone:

REQUIREMENT:

ASSUMPTIONS:

CONSTRAINTS:

REQUIRED RESOURCES:

FUNCTIONAL GROUPS PARTICIPATING:

TOOL 2.1. Requirements Record

REQUIREMENTS RECORD

Project Title: The Jacksonville Company Management Information System

Project Manager: Michael James   **Date:** May 14, 2007

Customer: The CEO, ABC Company

Customer Contact: Jason Burns   **Contact Phone:** 770-654-7000 x432

REQUIREMENT: A Management Information System (MIS) to support a corporate office consisting of 50 people. The MIS will produce forms, reports, data, and analyses specified by the Information Systems Department's needs analysis (MIS Needs Analysis, dated January 30, 2007). The MIS will be operational no later than April 1, 2008.

ASSUMPTIONS: The following assumptions have been made in determining the resource requirements for this project:
- Jack Smith will be assigned as the technical lead for the project
- Jean Jordan and Bill Williams will be available 50% of their time to support the project manager with clerical and financial assistance
- The IS Department will complete its technology assessment by June 1, 2007
- This project has priority 1 status

CONSTRAINTS:
- Given the number of competing projects at Jacksonville, the schedule can be met only with complete functional area support of resources and materials
- A budget of $200,000 may be insufficient to support IS's technology recommendations

REQUIRED RESOURCES:
- Technical lead
- Two full-time programmers
- One part-time programmer
- Two design engineers
- One systems engineer

FUNCTIONAL GROUPS PARTICIPATING:
- Engineering
- Information Systems
- Software Development

TOOL 2.1a. Sample Requirements Record

I. Scope
II. Background
III. Applicable Documents
IV. Specifications
V. Standards
VI. Industry/Organizational Documents
VII. Other Documents
VIII. Requirements
IX. General Project Description
X. Detailed Project Requirements
XI. Systems Engineering
XII. Systems Analysis and Control
XIII. Baseline Generation
XIV. Software Design
XV. Hardware Design
XVI. Training Design, Delivery, and Installation
XVII. Concept of Operations
XVIII. Maintenance/Customer Support
XIX. Design Reviews
XX. System Requirements Review
XXI. System Design Review
XXII. Program Management
XXIII. Program Management System
XXIV. Risk Assessment, Mitigation, and Management Program
XXV. Life Cycle Cost Analysis and Control
XXVI. Program Electronic Database
XXVII. Acceptance Criteria
XXVIII. General Guidelines
XXIX. Buyer's Measure of Acceptability
XXX. Product Demonstration Milestones
XXXI. Test/Review Requirements
XXXII. Provider's Responsibility for Demonstrating Product Acceptability
XXXIII. Reporting Requirements
XXXIV. Review Meetings
XXXV. Status Reports

TOOL 2.2. Statement of Work

_____   1. Is the project consistent with our core business?

_____   2. Will the project meet or further our corporate goals?

_____   3. What experience gaps do we have in the organization?

_____   4. What technical gaps do we have in the organization?

_____   5. What personnel gaps do we have in the organization?

_____   6. What do we know about the customer/stakeholders?

_____   7. What does the customer know about us?

_____   8. Would a team member (another organization or company) improve our chances of winning the contract (successfully completing the project) by enhancing our internal capability or improving our credibility with the customer?

_____   9. Should our company be the prime contractor or a subcontractor?

_____   10. Who is our competition?

_____   11. What are the competition's strengths and weaknesses?

_____   12. Do we have the resources to meet this project's requirements?

_____   13. What is the probability of winning the contract or starting the project?

_____   14. What is the probability of successfully completing the project?

_____   15. What is the start-up cost of this project (writing the proposal and gearing up to initiate the project)?

TOOL 2.3.   Checklist for Making a Bid/No-Bid Decision

Project Name:	Project Control No.:	Preparer Name:	Preparer Signature:
Customer:	Customer Contact:	Contact Phone:	Date Prepared:

	Stakeholder Power Level (scoring: high = 10, medium = 5, low = 1)			Stakeholder's Interest in Project (on a scale of 1–10 with 1 being strongly against)			
	A Influence Over Others	**B** Direct Control of Resources	**C**	**D** Against or Neutral	**E** Supports Project	**F** Overall Stakeholder Ranking	Strategies for Moving "Against" and "Neutral" Stakeholders to Be Positive Supporters of the Project
Stakeholder Name	Influence Strength (1–10)	Influence Strength (1–10)	Score (Col A × Col B)	Score Strength (0%–50%)	Score Strength (60%–100%)	Score (Col C × Col D or E)	
1.							
2.							
3.							
4.							
5.							
6.							
7.							
8.							
9.							
10.							
11.							
12.							

Note: (1) In columns D and E, estimate how much the stakeholder is against or for the project. (2) In column F, the highest scores generally indicate the most powerful and most interested stakeholders, but it is important to flag the most powerful stakeholders who are the most against the project. (3) Develop strategies to move those stakeholders who are against the project into the "Supports Project" column.

TOOL 2.4.   Stakeholder Assessment Worksheet

TOOLS FOR CHAPTER 3: WORK BREAKDOWN STRUCTURE AND BASELINE DEVELOPMENT

The two most common work breakdown structure (WBS) formats are graphic and indented. Tool 3.1 shows the graphic format. This format is an excellent communication tool because it is visual. The disadvantages of this format are that it requires a lot of print space and most project management software programs do not support it. Tool 3.2 shows the indented format. This format is the most commonly used, although it is not particularly good for communicating project content or scope, at least compared with the graphic format, although it is easier to enter more detailed information into this format type.

Tool 3.3 is an integrated WBS that combines the WBS task listings with the various organizational categories of costs. This template can be easily developed in Microsoft Excel or other spreadsheet programs, and the headings can be changed to reflect the activities/functions of an organization. It is also an excellent tool for collecting all the costs of a project. Other tools that aid in this process are discussed in the section on tools for Chapter 6.

Remember that if something is not in the WBS, it is not in the project. Also, the WBS is usually the first place that potential risks can be identified.

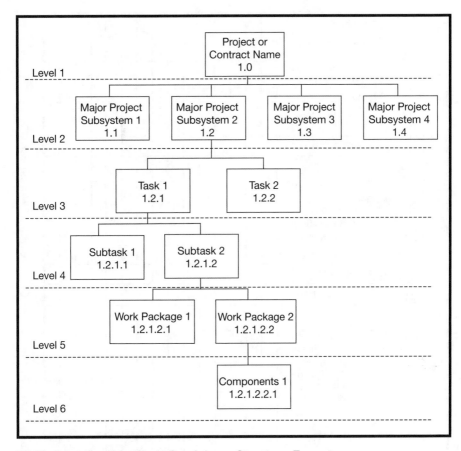

TOOL 3.1.   Graphic Work Breakdown Structure Format

WBS Number	Description		WBS Level
1.0 Project or Contract Name			1
1.1 Major Project Subdivision			2
1.1.1 Task			3
1.1.1.1 Subtask			4
1.1.1.1.1 Work Package			5
1.1.1.1.1.1 Components			6

TOOL 3.2.   Indented Work Breakdown Structure Format

Project: _____
Project Manager: _____

Estimator: _____
Date of Estimate: _____

Page _____ of _____

WBS No.	WBS Description	01 Engineering Labor	02 Manufacturing Labor	03 Systems Engineering	04 Facilities	05 Purchased Parts	06 Test Equipment	07 Tooling	08 Configuration Management	09 Software Development	10 Hardware Development	11 Integration and Assembly	12 Quality Assurance	13 Test	14 Subcontracts	15 Packaging	16 Integrated Logistics Support	17 Project Staff & Administrative Support	18 Graphics Support	19 Reproduction	20 Shipping and Handling	21 Consultants	Cost Account Totals	Total Project Cost

TOOL 3.3. Integrated Work Breakdown Structure, Work Package, and Cost Accounts Worksheet

TOOLS FOR CHAPTER 4: SCHEDULING

Tool 4.1 depicts the relationship of the WBS to the network diagram. It is important that the network diagram is developed using the lowest level of the WBS. Although it is possible to develop network diagrams from higher level WBS activities, if a problem area is discovered (e.g., a potential risk or overassigning resources), it is not possible to determine which task or tasks caused the problem unless the network diagram shows the lowest possible WBS level.

Tool 4.2 depicts a scheduling and cost-estimating process. It is important to determine the schedule first in order to determine the number of and skill sets of the resources. Once the schedule is set, other budgetary issues can be resolved.

Tool 4.3 shows the process of crashing a schedule. Crashing a schedule means looking at individual tasks on the critical path to determine the feasibility of reducing their duration. Usually, that means adding more people to a task. The rule of thumb is to reduce a task by one time unit (i.e., one day, one week, and so on, based on the unit of duration used in the project). Every time the duration is reduced, the critical path must be recalculated, because reducing tasks on the critical path eventually will cause one or more new critical paths to be developed. It usually is not cost effective to crash a schedule to the point that a new critical path is created. Crashing a schedule adds costs, whereas fast-tracking (making previously sequential tasks parallel) adds risk.

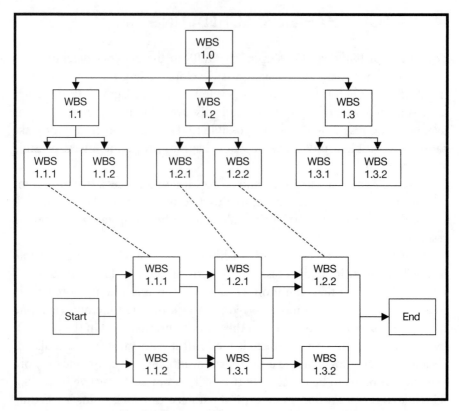

TOOL 4.1.   Relationship of the Work Breakdown Structure to Network Diagram

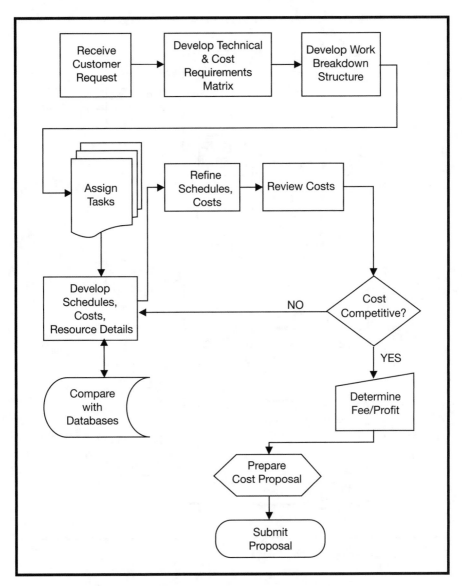

TOOL 4.2. Sample Scheduling and Cost-Estimating Process

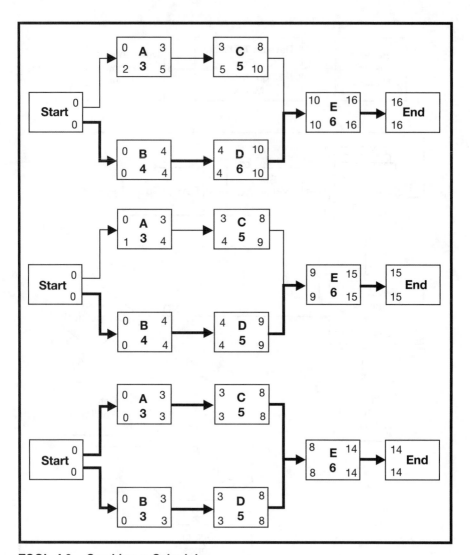

TOOL 4.3.   Crashing a Schedule

TOOLS FOR CHAPTER 5: COST CATEGORIES

Tool 5.1 shows the most common cost categories that a project manager deals with in any project. It is very important that the project manager understands each category and especially the distinction between direct and indirect costs. Many organizations try to force some of their indirect costs into a direct category in order to reduce overhead rates, but that practice is seldom successful and can lead to poor customer relations and loss of future projects

Tool 5.2 is a reminder of the inadequacies of many bidding processes. Although it is very costly to have a separate proposal group, the consequences of trying to use existing employees are shown in the table. Generally, the success rate of organizations that do not have a dedicated proposal group is around 15%.

Tool 5.3 is a flowchart of a generic cost-estimating process. Chapters 5 and 6 could logically be combined because they both discuss the overall process of cost estimating, the problems of estimating, and the results. More estimating tools are provided in the tools section for Chapter 6.

Direct costs
Indirect costs
Fixed costs
Variable costs
Semivariable costs
Other direct costs
Life cycle costs
Operating and maintenance costs

TOOL 5.1.   The Most Commonly Used Cost Categories

Problem	Consequences
■ Lack of historical project cost information	■ Each bid starts from scratch ■ There is no baseline for comparing previous failures or successes
■ Technical staff writes proposals as an additional duty	■ Technical staffs are not usually trained to assess or estimate costs
■ Outdated estimating database	■ Cost estimates are inaccurate
■ Reliance on intelligent guesses to estimate costs	■ Almost all estimates are too low; guesses compound the problem
■ Arbitrary cost changes by senior management	■ Even the most accurate cost estimates are negated ■ An unreasonable budget is created (usually too low), and profiles are minimized
■ Underused accounting systems	■ Reporting, database retrieval, and calculating systems are underutilized
■ Management secrecy in sharing labor and indirect rates	■ The staff's ability to assess alternative bidding strategies is reduced

TOOL 5.2. Inadequacies of Estimating, Costing, and Bidding Jobs

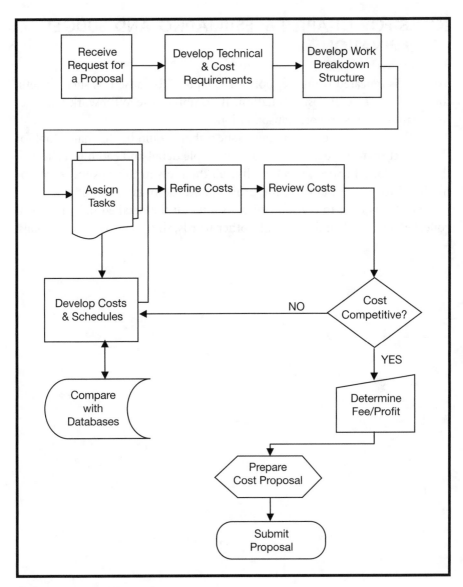

TOOL 5.3.   Cost-Estimating Process

TOOLS FOR CHAPTER 6: ESTIMATING AND BUDGET DETERMINATION

Tool 6.1 is repeated from the tools for Chapter 3 because it is such a useful tool in all aspects of cost estimation. It combines the WBS work packages in a way that aids in cost consolidation.

Tool 6.2 is a cost-estimating worksheet that should be the major tool for the project manager because it provides ample detail and room to collect all the cost data. Of course, this tool, like all the tools in this appendix, can be modified to fit the industry, the project, and the organization.

Tool 6.3 is used to consolidate costs after all the detailed information is collected, analyzed, and totaled. In other words, this form shows cost totals.

Project: _____
Project Manager: _____
Estimator: _____
Date of Estimate: _____
Page _____ of _____

WBS No.	WBS Description	01 Engineering Labor	02 Manufacturing Labor	03 Systems Engineering	04 Facilities	05 Purchased Parts	06 Test Equipment	07 Tooling	08 Configuration Management	09 Software Development	10 Hardware Development	11 Integration and Assembly	12 Quality Assurance	13 Test	14 Subcontracts	15 Packaging	16 Integrated Logistics Support	17 Project Staff & Administrative Support	18 Graphics Support	19 Reproduction	20 Shipping and Handling	21 Consultants	Cost Account Totals	Total Project Cost

TOOL 6.1. Integrated Work Breakdown Structure, Work Package, and Cost Accounts

Project Name:	Project Control No.:	Preparer Name:	Preparer Signature:
Customer:	Customer Contact:	Contact Phone:	Date Prepared:

RESOURCE REQUIREMENTS

Resource	Effort Duration	Availability for Project Work	Productivity (Assume 75% Productive)	Estimated Resource Effort (Time Devoted to Project)	Labor Rate	Resource Cost
					Total Labor Costs	

TOOL 6.2. Project Cost-Estimating Worksheet

MATERIALS COST		
Materials	**Unit Cost**	**Materials Costs**
Total Materials Cost		
OTHER DIRECT COSTS		
Other Direct Costs	**Unit Cost**	**Other Direct Costs**
Total Other Direct Costs		

TOOL 6.2. Project Cost-Estimating Worksheet Format (continued)

Project Name:	Project Control No.:	Preparer Name:	Preparer Signature:
Customer:	Customer Contact:	Contact Phone:	Date Prepared:

COST ESTIMATES			
Cost Category	**Unit Cost**	**Number of Units**	**Total Line Item Cost**
Direct Costs			
Labor			
Hardware			
Software			
Materials			
Equipment			
Administrative Support (Chargeable to Contract)			
Other Direct Costs			
Consultants			
Printing			
Equipment Rental			
Facility Rental			
Transportation Charges			
Travel			
Training			
Indirect Costs			
Employee Benefits			
General & Administrative			
TOTAL			

TOOL 6.3. Cost-Estimating Table

TOOLS FOR CHAPTER 7: PLANNING THE PROJECT

Tool 7.1 is the project plan outline. This outline can be adapted to any project in any industry. The importance of planning cannot be overemphasized. Notice that the project plan also generates many ancillary plans. One of the most important is the risk plan.

Tool 7.2 is a general risk identification worksheet. It is useful when identifying and collecting information about potential risks events. The purpose of this tool is to provide an organized way to collect risks according to whether they present an opportunity or a threat and rank them (high or low) in terms of impact and probability of occurrence.

Tool 7.3 provides a worksheet for determining and recording risk response strategies for both opportunities and threats.

Tool 7.4 is a contingency plan worksheet that aids in developing an overall risk plan.

Tool 7.5 is a risk evaluation form. It is used to keep track of how well response strategies are working and whether new response strategies need to be implemented.

I. Executive Summary
II. Management Summary
   A. Project Charter
   B. Project Scope
   C. Project Objective
   D. Narrative of Technical Solution
   E. Acceptance Criteria
   F. Contract Terms and Conditions
      1. Special Contract Requirements
      2. Third-Party Contract Conditions
   G. Budget and Other Financial Requirements
III. Project Requirements
   A. Statement of Work
   B. Work Breakdown Structure
IV. Deliverables
   A. Narrative Description
   B. Services
   C. Training/Operating Documents Required
V. Resource Requirements
   A. Internal
   B. Customer-Furnished Equipment
   C. Teaming/Vendor Requirements
   D. Project Team Skill Sets and Numbers
VI. Potential Project Risks
   A. Risk Assessment
   B. Mitigation Strategies
VII. Schedules
   A. Milestones
   B. Master Schedule
   C. Phase Schedule
   D. Data Delivery Schedule
   E. Meetings Schedule
VIII. Reporting Requirements
   A. Internal
   B. External
IX. Standards/Regulatory Requirements
X. Ancillary Plans
   A. Risk Plan
   B. Implementation Plan
   C. Communications Plan
   D. Hardware Development Plan
   E. Software Development Plan
   F. Configuration/Change Management Plan
   G. Logistics Plan
   H. Service and Maintenance Plan
   I. Quality Plan
   J. Subcontractor Management Plan
   K. Documentation/Training Plans

TOOL 7.1. Project Plan Outline

RISK IDENTIFICATION

Project Name:	Project Control No.:	Preparer Name:	Preparer Signature:
Sponsor:		Sponsor Phone:	Other Affected Stakeholders:	Date Prepared:

Risk ID No.	WBS No.	Risk Event Description	Person Assigned	Human Resources Needed	Labor Costs	Other Resource Costs	Risk Mitigation Strategy	Estimated Benefits of Strategy		Estimated Cost of Implementation	
								Schedule	Costs	Schedule	Costs

TOOL 7.2. Risk Identification Worksheet

RISK RESPONSE STRATEGIES

Project Name:	Project Control No.:	Preparer Name:	Preparer Signature:
Customer:	Customer Contact:	Contact Phone:	Date Prepared:

Opportunity Response Strategies

Risk Category (High, Medium, Low)	WBS No.	Opportunity Risk Event	Opportunity Response Strategies

Threat Response Strategies

Risk Category (High, Medium, Low)	WBS No.	Threat Risk Event	Threat Response Strategies

TOOL 7.3. Risk Response Strategies Worksheet

RISK MANAGEMENT CONTINGENCY PLAN			
Project Name:	Project Control No.:	Preparer Name:	Preparer Signature:
Customer:	Customer Contact:	Contact Phone:	Date Prepared:

Potential Risk Event Description:

Reasons Triggering the Risk Event:

Risk Triggers:

Contingency Strategies:

Strategy Effectiveness/Follow-up Plans:

TOOL 7.4.   Risk Management Contingency Plan Worksheet

RISK EVALUATION			
Project Name:	Project Control No.:	Preparer Name:	Preparer Signature:
Customer:	Customer Contact:	Contact Phone:	Date Prepared:

Opportunity Evaluation

WBS No.	Opportunity Event	Strategy	Progress (Give Date of Report)	Strategy Effectiveness

Threat Evaluation

WBS No.	Threat Event	Strategy	Progress (Give Date of Report)	Strategy Effectiveness

TOOL 7.5.   Risk Evaluation Form

TOOLS FOR CHAPTER 8: THE IMPLEMENTATION PHASE

Tool 8.1 is a status report format. Status reporting is important and required for successful project management. This format is adaptable for any industry and any organization.

Tool 8.2 is an outline for a sample risk management plan. Risk management is an ongoing endeavor throughout a project, and the tools for Chapter 7 can be used as a part of the risk management plan.

Tool 8.3 is a sample work order (sometimes referred to as a task order) or work order amendment form. This tool is necessary for each task that is required in a project. It serves as the task leader's statement of work.

STATUS REPORT

Project Name: Report Date:

Project Phase: Report Period:

Project Manager:

Summary of Progress for Period:

Problems Encountered and Action Taken:

Planned Activities for Next Reporting Period:

Anticipated Problems:

Recommendations:

TOOL 8.1. Status Report

RISK MANAGEMENT PLAN

   I. Project Name and Brief Scope Description
  II. Risk Management Methodology
 III. Roles and Responsibilities
 IV. Funding
   V. Risk Measurement and Interpretation Methodology
 VI. Levels of Risk Response Responsibility
 VII. Risk Communication Plan
VIII. Risk Tracking and Documentation
 IX. Appendices
     A. Risk Table
     B. Risk Response Plan

TOOL 8.2. Risk Management Plan

WORK ORDER/WORK ORDER AMENDMENT

Project Manager:	Contract No.:	Work Order No.:
Task Leader:	Amendment No.:	Date Issued:

By signing below, the Project Manager and the Task Leader acknowledge that this Work Order is issued under the provisions of the primary contract shown above. The services authorized are within the scope of services set forth in the *Purpose* of this contract. All rights and obligations of the parties shall be subject to and governed by the terms and conditions. Amendment(s) (if applicable) and the signed Primary Agreement, including any subsequent modifications, are hereby incorporated by reference.

Purpose

(Attach additional sheets if necessary)

Statement of Work

Deliverables and Due Date:

Deliverables are subject to review and approval by
the Project Manager prior to acceptance of the work.
(Attach additional sheets if necessary)

Start Date	End Date

Budget

Description/Task	Quantity	Unit (Hrs)	Unit Cost	Total
1			$	$
2			$	$
Business Objective Supported:	Project budget shall pay an amount not to exceed			$

Both the Project Manager and the Task Leader are responsible for ensuring work performed is within the scope of this Work Order or Work Order Amendment. The Project Manager must monitor proper compliance with the terms of this Work Order and applicable statutes and regulations. **IN WITNESS WHEREOF, the parties have executed this Work Contract.**

Task Leader Approval		Project Manager Approval	
Signature	*Date*	*Signature*	*Date*
Print Name		Print Name	
Phone	E-mail	Phone	E-mail

TOOL 8.3.   Sample Work Order/Work Order Amendment Form

TOOLS FOR CHAPTER 9: MONITORING AND CONTROL

Tool 9.1 depicts the components of contract pricing. Notice that the price or fee is not a part of the project budget. Also notice that the project manager usually controls a part of the budget in the form of the contingency reserve. Senior management always controls the management reserve.

Tool 9.2 lists the most important earned value formulas. Until the formulas have been used enough to be committed to memory, a project manager can use this table as a reminder of the definitions of earned value management terms and how to calculate the values needed for monitoring and controlling a project.

Tool 9.3 is a sample earned value management report. Most project management software programs include such reports, but it is important for an organization to agree on a standard format that will be used by all groups in the organization. This tool provides a generic basis from which such a standard report format can be developed.

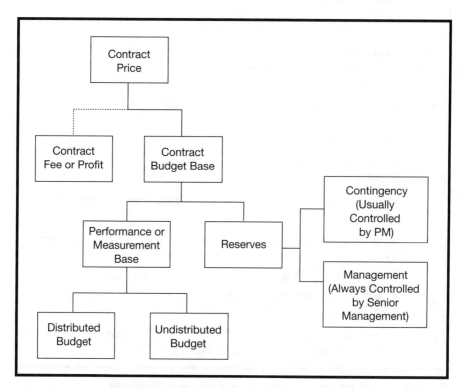

TOOL 9.1. Project Budget Components

Term	Definition	Formula
PV	**Planned value** of the work scheduled or the estimated cost of each task or project	PV for a project = total budgeted cost for each of the project tasks; PV for a task = total task budget
AC	**Actual cost** to accomplish the work or money expended to accomplish the EV	AC = total of all actual costs (labor, material, vendor, and subcontractor costs) at time of status checkpoint
EV	**Earned value** is the budgeted amount "earned" or completed against the planned amount	EV = (% of tasks completed) × PV of project or task
CV	**Cost variance** is the difference between the amount earned (EV) and the actual expenditures (AC)	CV = EV − AC
SV	**Schedule variance** is the difference between the amount accomplished or earned (EV) and the amount planned (PV)	SV = EV − PV
CPI	**Cost performance index** is a measure of the amount earned per each dollar expended	CPI = EV/AC
SPI	**Schedule performance index** is a measure of the physical work accomplished per each dollar expended	SPI = EV/PV
SAC	**Schedule at completion** is the total duration of the project schedule	SAC = total project schedule
BAC	**Budget at completion** is the total project cost	BAC = total project cost
ETC	**Estimate to complete** is the amount of money needed to finish a project from the point of each status checkpoint	ETC = BAC (or LRE) − AC
LRE	**Latest revised estimate** is the most recent budget estimate for total project cost	LRE = BAC (or previous LRE)/CPI
LRS	**Latest revised schedule** is the most recent estimate of total project duration	LRS = SAC (or previous LRS)/SPI

TOOL 9.2.   Earned Value Terms, Definitions, and Formulas

Reporting Period: _____ to _____

Project Name:	Project Control No.:	Preparer Name:	Preparer Signature:
Customer:	Customer Contact:	Contact Phone:	Date Prepared:

WBS Item No./Description	Current Period					Cumulative to Date					Estimate at Completion		
	Budgeted Cost		Actual Cost of Work	Variance		Budgeted Cost		Actual Cost of Work	Variance		Project Budget	Latest Revised Estimate	Variance
	Planned Value	Earned Value		Cost	Schedule	Planned Value	Earned Value		Cost	Schedule			

TOOL 9.3. Earned Value Report

Explanation of Variances:

Risks or Issues That Caused Variances:

Strategies to Correct Variances:

Expected Issues for the Next Reporting Period:

TOOL 9.3. Earned Value Report (continued)

TOOLS FOR CHAPTER 10: UNDERSTANDING THE PROJECT CHANGE PROCESS

Tool 10.1 is a standard change request form. It can be used by anyone who feels there is a need for a project change. Remember that all change requests must first go to the project manager, who either decides whether or not to implement the change, if that decision is within his or her authority, or passes it on to the change control board.

Tool 10.2 is the change control form. It is used to monitor a change action.

Tool 10.3 is a change responsibility form that shows who is involved in or impacted by a change. It helps the project manager keep track of the progress of a change as well as who is responsible for what action.

CHANGE REQUEST FORM

Document Preparation Information

Project Name:	Date Prepared:	Document File No.:

Prepared by:	Signature:

Project Background Information

Project Manager:	Change Request No.:	Date Requested:
Requester:	Requester Signature:	Dept./Title:
Phone:	E-mail:	Office No.:

Customer Information

Customer:	Contract Title and No.:	Contact Phone:

Proposed Change

Baseline Description:

Change Description:

Rationale:

Risks/Impact to Product/Project:

Other Work Breakdown Structure Activities Impacted

WBS No.:	Work Package Title/How Impacted:
WBS No.:	Work Package Title/How Impacted:
WBS No.:	Work Package Title/How Impacted:
WBS No.:	Work Package Title/How Impacted:

Approvals

Name (Printed):	Signature:	Date:
Name (Printed):	Signature:	Date:
Name (Printed):	Signature:	Date:

Product/Project Impact Review

Meeting Date/List of Attendees:

Technical/Architectural Impact:

Cost Impact:

Schedule Impact:

Performance/Quality Impact:

Contract Impact:

Change Control Board Action: ☐ **Approved** ☐ **Denied**

_____   _____
Signature, Change Control Board Chair   Date

Customer Action: ☐ **Approved** ☐ **Denied**

_____   _____
Signature, Customer   Date

TOOL 10.1. Change Request Form

CHANGE CONTROL FORM

Project Name:	Change Control Ref. No.:	Prepared by:	Preparer Signature:
Customer:	Customer Contact:	Contact Phone:	Date:

Initiator Information

Change Requester:	Requester's Title and Organization:
Phone:	E-mail:

Change Information

Nature of change:

Is change out of scope ☐ Yes ☐ No
If change is out of scope, complete the following.

Detail the technical impact of the proposed change:

Detail the cost impact of the proposed change:

Detail the schedule impact of the proposed change:

Change authority signature:

Change Control Board Chairman/Project Manager   Date

TOOL 10.2. Change Control Form

CHANGE RESPONSIBILITY FORM

Project Name:	Project Reference No.:	Prepared by:	Preparer Signature:
Customer:	Customer Contact:	Contact Phone:	Date Prepared:

Project Manager

Phone:	E-mail:	Office Location:

Responsibilities:

Customer Project Manager:

Phone:	E-mail:	Office Location:

Responsibilities:

Change Control Board (list members):

Responsibilities:

Other Stakeholder Interested Parties (list names):

Responsibilities:

TOOL 10.3. Change Responsibility Form

TOOLS FOR CHAPTER 11: SUCCESSFULLY CLOSING THE PROJECT

Tool 11.1 is a simple—but vital—checklist. Basically, the project team must do two audits: a technical audit to determine if all the project requirements have been met and an administrative audit to close out contract items, the project office, and so on. This checklist may not be applicable to every project, but it provides a basis for ensuring that the principal actions are completed. The checklist can be modified to fit an organization and an industry, and the project manager should ensure such a checklist exists when a project begins.

Project Name:	Project Control No.:	Preparer Name:	Preparer Signature:		
Customer:	Customer Contact:	Contact Phone:	Date Prepared:		
Closeout Activity			**Yes N/A No**	**Planned Closeout Date**	**Closeout Complete Date**
1. Obtain sign-off for deliverables			☐ ☐ ☐		
2. Update project plan for transfer to next project manager			☐ ☐ ☐		
3. Provide project staffing plan for reduced resource requirements if applicable			☐ ☐ ☐		
4. Write project turnover memo to all stakeholders			☐ ☐ ☐		
5. Perform postproject review: What worked well? What did not work well? What can be done to improve the next project?			☐ ☐ ☐		
6. Update project history file			☐ ☐ ☐		
7. Give individual performance feedback to team members			☐ ☐ ☐		
8. Close project accounts and finalize all billing			☐ ☐ ☐		
9. No claims or audits are pending on this project			☐ ☐ ☐		
10. All customer-provided equipment returned			☐ ☐ ☐		

TOOL 11.1. Project Closeout Checklist

INDEX